PRAISE FOR PROGRESSIVE

"Progressive Delivery is one of those practices that seems simple on the surface but whose waters run deep....Come for the practices, stay for the reframing of how to think about and improve your organization. *Progressive Delivery* just might be the catalyst that enables organizations to change."

—**Nathen Harvey**, DORA Lead and Developer Advocate, Google Cloud

"*Progressive Delivery* presents a working guide for people who are interested in building adaptively, responsibly, and agentically in the midst of rapid change....This approach centers human decision-making, clarity of purpose, and collaborative goals, which have too often been lacking from out-of-the-box technology approaches."

—**Dr. Cat Hicks**, Software Research Scientist, Catharsis Consulting

"This book is written by the strategists who pioneered Progressive Delivery...The text steps between the four pillars of a delivery framework and corresponding case studies from big real-world teams. Ultimately, this is a call to action on why tech has to serve up customer happiness and not just process metrics."

—**Alexis Richardson**, CEO and Cofounder, ConfigHub

"This book builds on existing paradigms and sage wisdom to introduce the concept of Progressive Delivery. Get your highlighter ready, there's some good stuff in here!"

—**Katie McLaughlin**, Senior Developer Relations Engineer, Google Cloud

"From thought leaders in the industry, an invigorating new model for how (and why) to deliver software."

PROGRESSIVE DELIVERY

PROGRESSIVE DELIVERY

Build The Right Thing   **For The Right People**   **At The Right Time**

James Governor, Kim Harrison,
Heidi Waterhouse & Adam Zimman

IT Revolution
Portland, Oregon

25 NW 23rd Pl, Suite 6314
Portland, OR 97210

First Edition
Printed in the United States of America
30 29 28 27 26 25   1 2 3 4 5 6 7 8 9 10

Cover and book design by D.Smith Creative, LLC

Library of Congress Control Number: 2025012420

Paperback: 9781950508976
Ebook: 9781950508983
Audio: 9781950508990

For information about special discounts for bulk purchases or for information on booking authors for an event, please visit our website at www.ITRevolution.com.

Dedication

To our families, for putting up with us.
To our friends, for encouraging us.
To our colleagues, for inspiring us.

CONTENTS

PREFACE

Like many good stories, this one begins with rage.

***

It's a Tuesday evening at 6:17 p.m. You're making dinner. Your phone rings and you answer. Your parents are in hysterics. "We're trying to transfer money between accounts, and we can't figure out how to log in to the bank website!" After a few minutes of calming them down and trying to understand the situation, you realize their bank rolled out a new website, moved the location of the login screen, and implemented mandatory multi-factor authentication. You spend the next two hours helping them navigate the new interface and set up an authenticator app on their phone. By this point your dinner has burned and cooled into a charred mass. Technology has jerked your parents forward.

***

It's Friday at 9:52 p.m. You open the app on your phone to adjust the alarm on the "smart" speakers in your bedroom and your children's rooms. You need to ensure you're all up to make it to the airport on time the next day for your flight to Boston. When the app opens, it's different. You think, "Oh, cool, a new update. Looks nice, lots of rounded corners, etc." Then you start looking for the alarm control settings. After twenty minutes of tapping on every section of the screen, you finally go to Google to find out where the alarm control moved to, only to learn through numerous Reddit threads that the new app removed all ability to see or change alarms in your system. The comments then inform you there is no way to revert or roll back the app version. You spend the next hour trying to set up alarm clocks in all the bedrooms without waking the kids, your partner, or the dog. Technology has jerked your family forward.

***

It's Monday at 8:27 a.m. You need to hop on a video call at 9 a.m. to prep your boss's boss for a meeting with the CEO about budget justification. You open the app for your video conference, and there is a pop-up window informing you that you need to update the app before continuing. You download the update, install it, and restart the app. You're able to get into the meeting at 9:06 a.m. and apologize for being late. You share a recap of the situation and are about to share your proposal when another pop-up window appears on your screen with the message, "For security and compliance, your computer will shut down and update in 3...2...1." By the time your laptop finishes updating, it is now 9:12 a.m. Your budget request was not approved. Why can't technology do a better job delegating control of when changes occur?

***

It's Wednesday at 9:41 a.m., and your CEO just flipped a feature flag for that cool new idea your team implemented from the main stage of your company's conference in front of a live audience of over five thousand users. Instantaneously, the user interface for hundreds of thousands of users changes. You've spent months working on this redesign, building and testing in production to ensure everything would work and had 100% feature parity. Over the next few hours, the reactions and reviews from users start to appear online. Half of the reviews are from happy users who love the new interface and find the enhancements intuitive. But the other half are from users who are frustrated because you changed the workflow they used. Some are even having legal challenges because of contractual obligations around training timelines. Within days you hear this divide is showing up in sales meetings with customers as well. Some companies love the new vision and direction, while others are threatening to cancel contracts because of the disruption the change caused to their business. You could roll back the new user experience for everyone, but then the happy users would be angry (they really like the new design). On the other hand, keeping it on risks losing the users who were not ready for the change. You want to deliver the right product, but the readiness for something new varies across your user base.

***

It's Friday at 04:09 UTC, and you push out a routine content configuration change to 100% of your globally distributed enterprise customers. Due to a bug in your content validation system, your change passed validation despite containing problematic content data. Within hours your change has caused the crash of 8.5 million devices. The resulting economic impact from this incident is estimated at $5.4 billion. Your development practices would benefit from a more progressive approach to software delivery.

***

These are just a few stories that we have lived where the rapidly increasing rate of change has led to a technological jerk felt by users. Where some might be justified in their frustration, we want to channel the rage and start to build the right product for the right people at the right time.

INTRODUCTION

For the past thirty years, technologists have spent an immense amount of time and effort getting better at making software. We have refined how we deliver it, how we support it, how we build it, how we store it, how we run it, and even how we talk about it. The cloud is our environment, and the network is our foundational metaphor.

Technologists can create miracles and wonders with software, but without a user, none of that matters. Without users, we can't make money, change the world, or provide anyone with any value. Users are the other side of the software delivery equation, and they often get overlooked or undervalued in the process.

All of the work we've done to improve the software creation and deployment process in the last thirty years is effectively invisible to the user. On one hand, this is good. We don't want to share our struggles with our customers. But what does this evolution in the software development life cycle look like from the user's perspective? Let's flip the mirror.

What looks like deployment from our side looks like a release from the user side. This release is essentially a demand, a push, from us to them that requires a change in *their* behavior. We may ask them to update, or we may thrust updates upon them. But unlike greatness, update notifications are very persistent. The more often we want users to accept our changes, the more change we ask them to adapt to, even if it's very tiny.

Progressive Delivery takes the DevOps idea of breaking the wall between silos to its logical conclusion: We need to knock down the wall between software *users* and software *makers*.

We already have the tools we need for this demolition—automation across all layers of the stack, configuration as code, monitoring, observability, telemetry, feature flags, security built into the software development life cycle (SDLC), and, yes, data collection.

We can see how people use our software, or don't, if we only care to look. Once we understand how users truly engage with our software, we can package and parse that knowledge and use it to create software that better fits the user's needs and desires. In other words, we can understand software in the context of it actually being used, not just designed.

In our thirty years of improving software delivery, the part we've been missing is how our software affects the people who use it. Figure 0.1 condenses all the very real and important technical advances of coding, testing, and shipping as "making software" (on the left) and expands out all the ways our users can interact with what we've made (on the right). On top are user behaviors and on the bottom are the tools we share with users to make those behaviors possible.

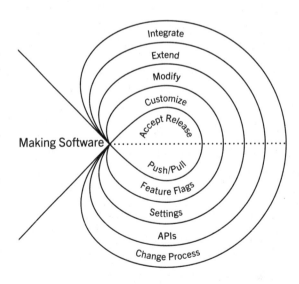

FIGURE 0.1: Software Acceptance and Use After Delivery

We, as software developers, are at the core, pushing or offering deployments and our users accepting them. Feature flags can customize the behavior of forcing or accepting changes. Settings can modify the software's environment. APIs can extend the program's data and behavior to a different format. Integration occurs when the user elects to use other software to interact with our software to meet their needs.

This *progression* reflects how the control point of software behavior shifts further away from the software creator (developer) and more toward the software consumer (user). It may seem counterintuitive that the "integrate/change process" is on the outer loop, since this seems pretty technical, but that's actually the point where our software interacts with the user's software. After all, our software is not the only tool our users are using to get their work done, so this ripple intersects with the ripples of dozens of other software products in the user's unique ecosystem (see Figure 0.2).

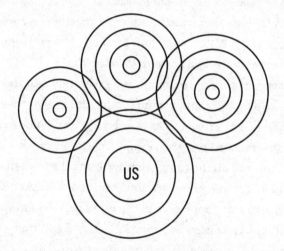

FIGURE 0.2: User's Software Ecosystem Has Many Interactions

Why We Wrote This

Any new way of describing the world requires context. It requires a community. It is a set of ideas and practices that are packaged up and it often has a moment that helps to crystallize things. The software industry has spent the last thirty years trying to get better at writing software.

We (the developer community) have talked about continuous delivery and Agile. We have gotten much better at testing and shifted testing left. We have done many things, but we have never managed to do them for everybody. We're always promising a bright future...if only. The community working on user-centricity in the future already needs to make it a mainstream phenomenon. To make this new model accessible, we must name it and talk about it.

In 2017, James Governor had an intuition based on a conversation with Sam Guckenheimer, who worked at Microsoft. After hearing about the application routing processes Microsoft used for rolling out services, James realized that one part of the puzzle, which Microsoft called "progressive experimentation," was really about a broader phenomenon—Progressive Delivery. The impact of a basket of technologies and approaches applies to the entire SDLC. From there, our group came together—James Governor, Adam Zimman, Heidi Waterhouse, and Kimberly Harrison—and began to talk about, contextualize, and advance these ideas.

We all have a history of communicating with multiple stakeholders in the industry, helping them understand complex ideas and make them more broadly applicable. We have decades of experience and now we're bringing it together to bear on this new idea. Progressive Delivery takes all the goodness of the cloud and all the things that were not there when some of the original works in continuous integration/continuous delivery (CI/CD) were written and makes them applicable for now and into the future.

With continuous delivery and even late-stage Agile, there was the idea of the separation of deployment from release. With Progressive Delivery, though, we are adding that larger community in the context of our consumer. In Progressive Delivery, we now have deployment, release, and adoption. (See Figure 0.3.) That user cycle is representative of adoption, and that is the part we need to incorporate back into how we're thinking about our software delivery. We've gotten significantly better at shipping software, but helping people adopt that software and feel good about it... that's where we need to do a lot of work.

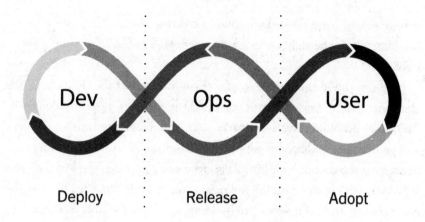

Deploy   Release   Adopt

FIGURE 0.3: Deployment vs. Release and Who's Impacted

As Dr. Cat Hicks notes, "A successful software builder wants to create a successful, positive relationship to the change they're introducing."[1] We want users involved and happy. The truth is that different people are going to adopt software at different paces, and we're always going to be in an environment that is a mixture of the old and the new.

The first key breakthrough is understanding that the cloud changed everything because of its opportunities to increase autonomy, alignment, abundance, and automation. Particularly abundance. There are things we could do with the cloud that we could never do before. But the second most important breakthrough, the crucial breakthrough, is closing the third loop. It's not enough to have DevOps as two loops; we need to bring the user into the heart of what we are doing. That is the prize and the opportunity. That's what makes Progressive Delivery different.

Who Should Read This Book

Progressive Delivery is a holistic framework for an entire organization. It is intended to bring together the business, the builders, and the users in a way that honors everyone. But change really starts at the source, the builders. This book is primarily written from the perspective of enabling software developers, who are at the front line of creating change, to create an environment where the right software gets delivered to the right people at the right time.

We say, "build the right thing for the right users at the right time." We start with "build" because until you build the software you can't deliver it. And how you build directly impacts your options at the time of delivery and your ability to observe adoption. Generative AI and vibe coding may be shifting the cost of building all variations to a nominal fee, but the cycle still starts with understanding the right thing to build. We need to start the conversation around how we are building to properly enable our teams to deliver to the right users at the right time.

Whether you are an engineering lead, a product owner, or an executive, this book is intended to expose you to the latest in software delivery thinking. Throughout the book, we also discuss how software creation and delivery affect other groups, who we call constituents (more on this below). We want to provide some useful ways to change your thinking about software delivery and some practical questions and techniques to make that delivery progressive, inclusive, and future proof.

When we talk about the collective of people who use and make our software and those who market, sell, and distribute it, we could use the traditional expression "stakeholders," but mostly, we prefer to think about that constellation of people as *constituents*.

- A **stakeholder** is a person who cares about the outcomes. In a very literal sense, stakeholders have a stake in the success of the product. This can be a developer whose job performance is tied to the product, an investor, or company management.
- A **constituent** is someone who contributes to success. This can include developers, support, marketing, users, and IT departments.

We need to treat users as participants in our work rather than as objects. We're doing something with them, not to them.

How to Read This Book

This book is a layer cake of theory and practice. The theory chapters provide explanations for what we are seeing in the industry, what you can look for in your organization, and questions to ask yourself about your alignment with Progressive Delivery. The corresponding case study chapters demonstrate a particular aspect of Progressive Delivery in action, but, of course, other elements also make their way in. Read through the book and focus on the parts that line up with your current experience. Then go through and use the questions at the end of the chapters to consider how you want to tweak the practices and behaviors in your organization.

Tools and Patterns

These tools and patterns are ways that we have seen organizations practice Progressive Delivery. Many of them flow into each other or relate to each other, but we are listing them in alphabetical order for ease of reference. We're introducing these concepts here as they'll come up throughout the book and form a foundation to engage in moving toward a Progressive Delivery approach.

Blast Radius

This is a way to describe how much effect a change will have. It is often coupled with ring deployment or canary deployments. Changes with a small blast radius limit the impact of changes since only a few people will be affected. Limiting the blast radius also provides an early feedback loop on changes from the user perspective.

Blue-Green Deployments

Blue-green deployments are often used in a "breaking change" scenario. If a software change is going to change how data is stored and communicated, the blue-green pattern helps prevent data loss. A second full system is set up that mirrors the original system, and traffic is directed to both systems simultaneously to check that the data is all being stored properly and that the new system is robust. Only then is the older system shut down. Variations on this pattern include load migration and traffic shaping. The pattern is also related to sunsetting.

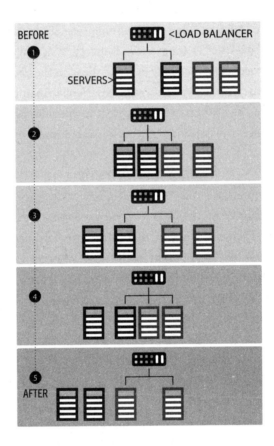

FIGURE 0.4: Progression of a Blue-Green Deployment

Canary Testing

Derived from the use of canaries in coal mines as an early warning for poor air quality, a canary test rolls out a software change to a small group of monitored users and checks their response and experience. In the coal mining story, the canary stops singing and faints if it loses oxygen. Since canaries are very small, it's a sensitive indicator. In the same way, canary testing is a sensitive test that can indicate general safety for the group, but only if it is well-monitored. Canary tests are often administered by feature flags and may be part of a ring deployment strategy.

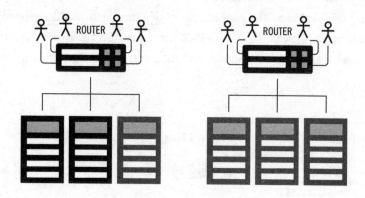

FIGURE 0.5: Canary Deployment

Used to Evaluate Viability of a Change Before Exposing to All Users

Constituents

Software is not just a set of computer instructions. It is a web of relationships between people, processes, and systems. The constituents of a Progressive Delivery system include the developers, the product team, the businesses that create and consume the software, the environment, and the users. For example, a healthcare record system is created by a product team and developers, sold by marketers and salespeople, maintained by operations and support staff, and used by insurance companies, healthcare providers, and patients. All those people are part of the constituency of the healthcare software.

Feature Flags

Feature flags are a way to change the behavior of software at runtime based on conditions that may be external to the code. Feature flags can be used to control software based on conditions such as user ID, browser language, geographic region, software version, security permission level, A/B testing cohort, and server.

Feature flags frequently fall into two categories: ephemeral flags, which are used for a finite period of time and then removed from the code base to prevent inadvertent activation, and long-lived flags, which control aspects of the software that will continue to be variable. For example, an ephemeral flag might control the phased rollout of a new feature. A long-lived flag might control software that has a paid premium tier. Feature management software helps organize, control, and distribute an organization's feature flags.

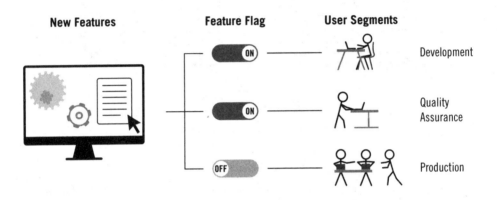

FIGURE 0.6: Feature Flag Controlling Which User Segments Have Access to a New Feature

Observability

Observability is the combination of gathering high-cardinality data about a system (including its users) and being able to ask unanticipated questions about that data.

Release Impact

Much like blast radius, release impact is a way to understand the effect of a software change. However, release impact also implies that the change may be positive. Some implementations of release impact also include a consideration of monetary effects.

Release vs. Deployment vs. Acceptance/Adoption

Deployment is the act of getting software to a place where it will be available to the users. Release is the point where users can actually use the software and are told about it. Acceptance or adoption is when users make the software a part of their workflows.

Ring Deployments

A ring deployment is the practice of deploying software to increasingly larger groups of people as part of a release strategy. For example, the first ring might be to the team, and the second ring might go to 1% of the users, then 10% of the users, etc. At each stage, the impact is evaluated.

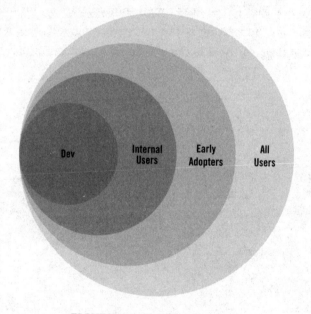

FIGURE 0.7: Ring Deployment

Rollbacks

One way to make changes less dangerous is to ensure that they can be reverted cleanly. Controlling releases with feature flags makes it faster and easier to roll back to a previous state without needing to change code, especially in an urgent situation. As Thomas Dohmke, CEO of GitHub, said in an interview with us: "The feature flag is only really useful if you can't only progressively roll out, but you also need to be able to aggressively roll back. That's actually the key feature."[2]

Test in Production

In a complex modern software environment, it is impossible to fully test every scenario before software is released. However, production is a test environment from which we can obtain valuable information if we choose to record and integrate it.

Sunsetting

All software has a lifespan. When software needs to be retired, some users are ready to move on to the next thing, and some aren't, for business or personal reasons. Sunsetting is the act of retiring software or versions using feature flags so there is not an abrupt cutoff but a mindful wind down.

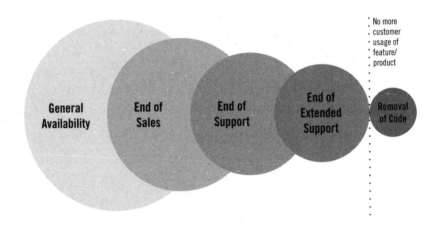

FIGURE 0.8: Software End-of-Life Diagram

Progressive Delivery Is a Mindset

Empowering the user to change their experience of software is an extension of the Agile, DevOps, and CI/CD philosophies. Our collaboration circle grows wider as our ability to understand and incorporate data increases. From the organizational side, abundance, autonomy, alignment, and automation make it easier for organizations to create and sustain software that is flexible, responsive, and useful.

We believe that with this guide, you will be able to look at your own organization and see places where you can improve one of the four A's and thus deliver value a little sooner or more accurately or make the work with others easier.

Chapter 1
PROGRESSIVE DELIVERY

"Well, in our country," said Alice, still panting a little, "you'd generally get to somewhere else—if you run very fast for a long time, as we've been doing."

"A slow sort of country!" said the Queen. "Now, here, you see, it takes all the running you can do, to keep in the same place. If you want to get somewhere else, you must run at least twice as fast as that!"

—**Lewis Carroll**, *Through the Looking-Glass and What Alice Found There*

In physics, a jerk isn't just someone cutting you off in traffic—it's the rate at which acceleration changes. Technically known by physicists as the third derivative of position, it's the feeling that makes you grab for the subway pole when the train lurches or brace yourself during an elevator's sudden start. It's that moment when steady, predictable motion becomes a jolt, defying your expectations of smooth acceleration.

> **jerk (/jurk/):** The rate of change of an object's acceleration over time.

We feel this same jerk in our digital lives, where change itself is accelerating. The history of technology has been hallmarked by an ever-increasing velocity of transformation.

As Alvin Toffler warned in 1970, change is "a concrete force that reaches deep into our personal lives, compels us to act out new roles, and confronts us with the danger of a new and powerfully upsetting psychological disease." He called this phenomenon "future shock,"[1] and nothing in our current environment suggests the pace Toffler found dizzying fifty years ago will slow down.

These technological jerks reshape our personal worlds in profound ways. For someone born in the 1940s, a telephone represents stable technology—pick it up, dial, talk. For those born in the 2000s, the "phone" function might be the least-used app on their device. Everything from how we get our news to how we pay for coffee has become a digital experience that updates without warning, consent, or control. The global infrastructure we built in the twentieth century—networks of satellites, fiber-optic cables, and physical goods transfer—has compressed adoption timelines from decades to months. (See Figure 1.1.)

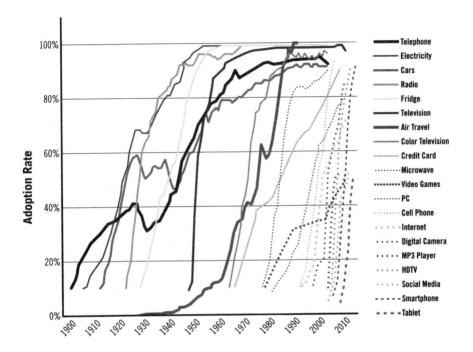

FIGURE 1.1: Adoption Rate of New Technologies from 1900 to 2012

Source: "The Topic We Should All Be Paying Attention to (in 3 Charts)," BlackRock Blog, December 11, 2015, https://web.archive.org/web/20160304140915/https://www .blackrockblog.com/2015/12/11/economic-trends-in-charts/.

In 1962, Everett Rogers captured the varied human response to this technological acceleration in *Diffusion of Innovations*, mapping out how new technologies ripple through society—from eager innovators who embrace the bleeding edge to early adopters, then the early and late majorities, and, finally, the cautious laggards who hold onto the familiar.[2] Geoffrey Moore later expanded this insight in *Crossing the Chasm*, revealing the treacherous gap between early enthusiasm and mainstream acceptance.[3]

Yet our relationship with change isn't simple. A developer might be the earliest adopter of a new operating system on their phone but continue to use a code editor that was built in 1976.* We are all early adopters in one area but laggards in another, picking our way through an increasingly complex technological landscape.

In our professional lives, these jerks multiply. Software dashboards proliferate—one for time tracking, another for performance metrics, and yet another for project management. Each makes perfect sense to its creators, but collectively they create a dizzying acceleration. When we ask colleagues to adapt to interface changes, we're asking them to absorb another jerk in their already dynamic workflow.

Organizations feel these forces of change even more acutely. They must innovate rapidly to stay competitive—ask Sears about the cost of failing to adapt to Amazon—while managing the increased risks of outages, user frustration, and business disruption. Traditional change management systems excel at handling smooth, predictable acceleration but falter when confronting these technological jerks.

The solution isn't to slow down—it's to give people more control over their rate of change. Every time we allow users choice, whether in personal tools or workplace software, we enable them to manage their own acceleration. Some choices can be elegantly wrapped—such as advanced settings hidden behind a simplified interface—making people partners in the software experience rather than subjects of it.

This is where Progressive Delivery comes in: a methodology that recognizes different users need different rates of change. As software builders, we can release as quickly as we want while letting users choose when to incorporate changes into their lives and workflows. It's about building systems that are both dynamic and respectful, systems that recognize the human need to sometimes grab the pole and steady ourselves before the next technological jerk arrives.

---

* Both "vi" and "Emacs" were first created in 1976 and remain two of the most popular code editing applications today.

The cost of mismanaging rollouts is all around us. Microsoft found itself forced to extend Windows 10 support when organizations balked at upgrading to Windows 11.

A tiny npm package called left-pad created a cascading failure that affected thousands of projects. A security company called CrowdStrike, which tens of thousands of organizations relied on, caused a major outage by pushing a breaking misconfiguration to 100% of their audience all at once. The cost of poor software delivery practices can run into the billions. It gets kind of expensive when the entire airline industry is grounded. These cases demonstrate what happens when rollouts are not effectively managed. And, really, as an industry, we should be doing better by now.

The signs of this mismatch are clear in any organization: declining user engagement, unused new features, the proliferation of third-party workarounds, and spikes in support requests. But these symptoms also point toward solutions. By understanding how different users and organizations absorb change—from early adopters to cautious laggards—we can create systems that respect their varying needs for stability and innovation.

Over the past century, we've seen adoption rates for new technologies compress dramatically. While television, computing, and other technologies required decades to reach mass adoption, the latest software-driven innovations can become mainstream in months (see Figure 1.2). This acceleration isn't slowing down—just look at ChatGPT.

As software builders, we're both agents and victims of this acceleration. Our code is just one thread in a vast tapestry of interdependent systems, each evolving at its own pace. When we push changes too fast or too frequently, we risk creating that jarring moment—that technological jerk—for our users. The impact depends on how quickly they're already adapting to change: What feels like a gentle nudge to an early adopter might throw a late majority user off balance entirely. We are not the only ones asking our users to adapt to changes—they use more than just our software, both at work and at home.

Throughout this chapter, we'll explore how Progressive Delivery provides a framework for managing technological change that respects both the need for innovation and the human experience of adaptation. By understanding how to deliver the right changes to the right users at the right time, we can turn the jarring experience of technological jerk into a more controlled and intentional acceleration. Let's start by examining exactly what Progressive Delivery means in practice and how it emerged as a response to these challenges.

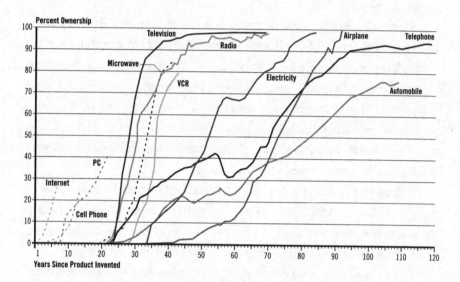

FIGURE 1.2: Years Since Technology Introduction to Reach Mass Ownership

Source: Federal Reserve Bank of Dallas, *1996 Annual Report: The Economy at Light Speed*, https://web.archive.org/web/20161224074319/https://www.dallasfed.org/~/media/documents/fed/annual/1999/ar96.pdf.

Toward a Practice of Progressive Delivery

Everywhere we look, we find new devices and services that offer replacements or enhancements to every aspect of our lives. But with these improvements come new challenges. If your device or application doesn't work, how does it get fixed? How long does it take? What if that software is running in your car? Or the locks on your house? Or the pump for your insulin? Is your software doing what you need, when you need it?

Different stakeholders want to move at different rates—factories want to run consistently all year, but consumers have times when they want to buy back-to-school clothes or holiday presents. Software developers want to be able to show delivered products before their performance reviews. Sales teams are driving toward quarterly and yearly goals. These stakeholders need a way to collaborate, not just coexist.

At its core, **Progressive Delivery is a set of software delivery practices to deliver the right software to the right users at the right time in a way that is sustainable for everyone.** Yes, everyone. This includes executives in the boardroom, leaders managing departments, engineers, designers, product teams, marketers, partners, and, most importantly, the actual product users. While this book is focused on software developers and how they can benefit from Progressive Delivery methods, Progressive Delivery is for all these stakeholders and constituents.

Progressive Delivery is not about tools or certifications. It's about what you care about and where your organization places focus. It's more of a lens than a prescription. Products are not static entities but thriving conversations where building, use, and retirement are all visible and trackable.

From a more nuanced perspective, Progressive Delivery can mean different things for different constituents:

- For the user or consumer of technology, Progressive Delivery is a user experience that minimizes technological jerk.
- For the company delivering a digital experience, Progressive Delivery is a set of practices that enable teams to move at a sustainable pace.
- For those tasked with building and delivering modern software, Progressive Delivery is a development practice that builds upon the core tenets of continuous integration and continuous delivery (CI/CD).

Progressive Delivery specifically adds two core tenets to that of CI/CD:

1. **Release progression:** progressively increasing the number of users who can see (and are impacted by) new features.
2. **Radical delegation:** progressively delegating the control of access to a feature to the owner who is closest to the outcome.

In essence, Progressive Delivery is the practice of delegating control to the user while retaining a clear vision and plan for the product. It's a way to understand what you're already doing regardless of the technology change happening in front of you, so you can do it more effectively.

Progressive Delivery asks the following key questions:

- What is "finished?" When is a product or feature truly complete, and how do we define success?
- What do we expect to happen? What are our hypotheses about how users will interact with the new features?
- What if users want a different cadence of change? How do we accommodate diverse user preferences?
- How are we stewarding the information we collect? How do we gather and analyze user feedback?
- How are we incorporating feedback? How do we use feedback to improve the product?
- Who are *all* of our constituents? We must recognize and consider the needs of all stakeholders, not just the loudest voices.

In the history of software development, Progressive Delivery represents the logical next step in a long line of improvements. According to Carlos Sanchez, who wrote the following while working at CloudBees:

> Progressive Delivery is the next step after Continuous Delivery, where new versions are deployed to a subset of users and are evaluated in terms of correctness and performance before rolling them to the totality of the users and rolled back if not matching some key metrics.[4]

Figure 1.3 shows the evolution of software development methods. While not comprehensive, it shows how our understanding of delivery can be additive. Specification-driven delivery (also known as waterfall) plus Agile gets us test-driven delivery (TDD). When we add operations and maintenance into the scope of TDD, we get DevOps. Adding automation to DevOps results in CI/CD. Progressive Delivery includes all the former models the way a pearl encapsulates its former layers.

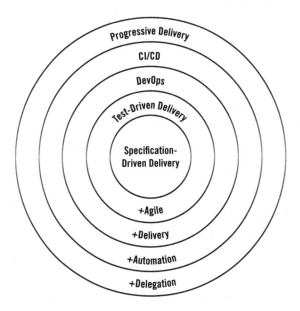

FIGURE 1.3: The Evolution of Software Development Methods

Of course, as software makers have been optimizing how to build software—through innovations in tooling and craft with continuous delivery and DevOps practices—they have exacerbated the problem of user adoption. Even if a team can *deploy* on demand, a user probably will not *adopt releases* multiple times a day.

This is the crux of why users are feeling the technological jerk now more than ever—adoption is about release cadence, not build cadence, but not all our systems are designed to separate those. The essential added ingredient in Progressive Delivery is delegation closer to the user.

This is how we continue down the path of high developer autonomy. We build systems that decouple deployment from release, and release from adoption, so users can operate at a more comfortable speed.

Once you start seeing the world in terms of Progressive Delivery, you see it everywhere—ripe mangoes in Midwest supermarkets and tap-to-pay parking meters, Calendly links, and same-day electronics delivery. User demand drives and encourages changes to delivery infrastructure. Consider Calendly: Setting up a meeting with someone used to require several steps, including figuring out availability for each person. By creating software to allow each user to independently choose a time, booking meetings has become faster and easier.

On the provider side, this coordination requires calendar rules, time zone awareness, email integration, and meeting location options. Similarly, delivering fresh tropical fruit to Minnesota in February requires a sophisticated transportation and distribution network and fruit varietals that are sturdy enough to ship and store. To the user, Progressive Delivery looks like convenience. But to a provider, Progressive Delivery takes a combination of investment, will, and effort.

The Four A's: A Framework for Progressive Delivery

The evolution of Progressive Delivery has been shaped by technological advances, much as physics has evolved to measure and manage forces of motion. Just as physicists use measurements of jerk to understand sudden changes in acceleration, there are four essential factors that help us measure and manage the technological jerks in our system: the four A's—abundance, autonomy, alignment, and automation. The rise of virtualization, containerization, and cloud computing led to the abundance of computing and storage resources. This abundance of resources led to increased developer autonomy, which was further accelerated by Git, distributed contribution, feature flags, and the architecture trend from monoliths toward microservices.

As autonomy increased, so did the need for focus and alignment. Teams began to prioritize—and value—API-first development and enhanced observability. This more loosely coupled architecture led to both the opportunity and the need for more automation and better feedback loops to manage the vast increase in the scale of systems and the opportunity to better understand user behavior and needs.

We can express this relationship as an equation:

$$Progressive\ Delivery\ =\ \frac{(Abundance \times Autonomy)}{(Alignment \times Automation)}$$

Abundance and autonomy form the foundation of the developer experience, much like the electrical grid supports our modern life. The fluctuations of power generation and conduction are smoothed out, and we get steady, reliable resources to use. We then get to choose how to apply the power streaming into our homes and businesses so abundantly. In the same way, abundance and autonomy in software development allow us to think about more difficult and interesting problems. However, just as we use everything from circuit breakers to dimmer switches to control the flow of power, the forces of abundance and autonomy also need to be well-regulated to be useful and safe.

Your "goal" for Progressive Delivery is to balance your abundance and autonomy by leveraging alignment and automation. If abundance and autonomy are too pronounced compared to alignment and automation, teams tend to build brittle systems filled with features that never get used. Conversely, if you focus too much on the user experience without addressing developer needs, you end up knowing what the users need, but you are unable to deliver it quickly enough.

In this way, abundance and autonomy are all about the developer experience, or the building side of a product, while alignment and automation are centered on the user experience, or the delivery of the product. We could simplify this as:

$$Progressive\ Delivery\ =\ \frac{Developer\ Experience}{User\ Autonomy}$$

If abundance and autonomy are the electrical grid, delivering us power and potential, then alignment and automation are the appliances that transform that energy into value. Voltage on a power line is not useful until we can convert it into light, heat, work, or video gaming minutes. Too much power and there's a risk to safety and property. Too little and we can't turn on a light or keep food cold. Alignment is what directs the current the way we want it. Automation makes our homes run without intervention and keeps us safe from mistakes or sudden surges. Without alignment and automation, we would be at risk of surprises or unwanted changes.

Let's examine each of these four pillars in detail:

Abundance

Abundance is a very large quantity of all the resources required to accomplish a task. In the context of Progressive Delivery, this centers around the developer experience. When building digital systems, this can be divided into compute resources, network bandwidth, and storage.

We can measure abundance both quantitatively (for example, how long it takes to provision a server or database for a new project) and qualitatively (for example, through developer surveys and interviews). Developer experience and abundance are interlinked. Abundance enables developers to work without friction and without waiting for permission to access resources.

Autonomy

Autonomy is the ability of an individual to act independently from others. When developing software, this independence means access to all necessary resources to complete a desired task. To have a Progressive Delivery environment, developers need to be able to innovate and build at their own pace.

To measure autonomy quantitatively, we can track how frequently developers are "blocked" or waiting for others to do their work. During some stages of growth or product expansion, the rate of blocking may naturally increase. We can also gain qualitative assessment through internal surveys.

Alignment

Alignment means focusing human and organizational resources responsible for developing software to work in the same direction. In Progressive Delivery, alignment is one of the two ways to wrangle abundance and autonomy. Both alignment and automation are centered around the user experience.

We can measure alignment through qualitative user surveys and interviews, as well as by monitoring usage rates and patterns in feature adoption and workflow completion. The exact method for gathering quantitative and qualitative data about user impact will vary with the software and the users, but it should be as broad as the team can afford, in order to capture multiple insights.

Automation

Automation is the identification and implementation of programmatic processes for repetitive tasks. For Progressive Delivery, automation is the second way to focus on abundance and autonomy. Automation supports alignment by intentionally looking for repetitive manual tasks and creating code to reduce effort while ensuring consistency. After all, one of the goals of computing, and now AI, is to make automation easier and more effective. Adoption is easier when it's automated and part of the workflow.

Measuring automation can be done quantitatively through observability tooling, which looks at the frequency of pattern repetition as users navigate a workflow. Qualitatively, user surveys can target questions about repetition and "too many steps" to accomplish frequent tasks.

Balancing Developer and User Experience

The benefit to adopting Progressive Delivery is that it is not an abrupt transformative moment but an evolution that works with what you're already doing well and gives you pointers to what could be improved. The cost of a "transformation initiative" is often denoted in millions, and the outcome may not be at all aligned to benefit the people who are implementing the changes and those consuming the result.

Just as electrical engineers need to balance variable generation and transmission with safe, reliable, controlled delivery, Progressive Delivery works to balance the surge and ebb of developer innovation with the measured and incremental pace of user acceptance. The goal is not to eliminate change or even acceleration, but to make it as smooth and acceptable as possible. The separation between deployment and release acts as a transformer, modulating the flow down to something a household can use safely, while still retaining the capacity to serve other households.

Progressive Delivery addresses the challenge of the pace of innovation by making a hard separation between the deployment of code to the production environment and the release of features to users. This separation allows for the business to have two priorities that are loosely coupled: developer autonomy and user adoption. (See Figure 1.4.)

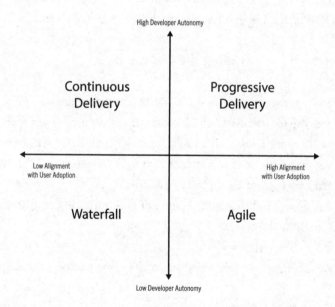

FIGURE 1.4: How Software Development Life Cycles Balance Developer Autonomy with User Adoption

Motivation and Sustainable Growth

Similarly, product teams as a whole need to know that there is a user demand for what they are building, and companies need to be able to situate themselves in an ecosystem of production and consumption. All of this alignment is much easier when the goal is something that can be communicated to everyone.

Dan Pink's *Drive* posited that humans are intrinsically motivated by autonomy, mastery, and purpose.[5] This theory fits well with what we know about burnout from Dr. Christina Maslach's work, where lack of autonomy and purpose and conflicts in moral values create a kind of moral injury.[6] Being able to connect our labor to the value that other people find in our work is a known way to stay engaged and happy.

We know that stasis is dangerous for companies—if you're not in touch with how your environment is changing, you're at a high risk of being passed by a competitor or becoming irrelevant. We also know that growth at all costs is a risky goal, especially in a post-ZIRP* world. Company growth needs to be sustainable or have sustainability on the horizon.

Finding the Middle Road

There are so many business metrics out there, and while we will give you a few more, the metric is not the goal any more than the map is the territory. If we measure people on something easily measured without repeatedly asking why they need to increase that measurement and the intended effect, then we get compliance but not cooperation.

So how do we find that middle road of making something useful, flexible, and sustainable?

- By delivering the right product to the right person at the right time.

---

* ZIRP: zero-interest-rate phenomenon. In this case, the behavior of companies when it is effectively free to borrow money. Although associated with the economic term *zero-interest-rate policy*, it is specific to how low borrowing costs affected risk estimation around investing in software and venture-backed startups.

- By avoiding overbuilding and over-optimizing.
- By working with the resources easily available.
- By making sure that we are addressing real needs our users value, not just what the loudest people are asking for.

If change is an inevitable part of our lives, both as producers and consumers, how do we make that change meaningful and useful instead of pointless motion without progress? To answer that question, we need to know what the point is—what are we trying to accomplish with what we're making, and what are the people who use it trying to accomplish? Without these purposes clearly in mind, we can never be sure that we're making the right thing.

Conclusion

Each of the four A's of Progressive Delivery reinforces and enables progress in the others. None of them is something that can be fully finished. Moore's Law continues to provide an abundance of resources. You can always automate a little more, or a realignment will reveal a way for a team to become more autonomous. Even autonomy continues to increase and expand in the face of coding assistants.

Change is a part of our lives every day. We tend to think of it as good change, like increases in capacity or learning, or bad change, like aging and decay. Change is stressful because it forces us to learn new habits and patterns and ways of doing things. The larger and faster a change is from a single point of view, the harder it is to adapt to it. Jared Spool, cofounder of Center Centre, said in the article "The Quiet Death of the Major Re-Launch,"

There's another way to build a new architecture with a whole new site without the risks of a re-launch....I explained that re-launches are a thing of the past. There was a time when sites launched in cycles, living from one major redesign to the next. Each new redesign would bring a whole new look, a whole new user experience....However, the best sites have replaced this process of revolution with a new process of subtle evolution. Entire redesigns have quietly faded away with continuous improvements taking their place.[7]

The way we build software has evolved to make it trivial to push changes to our users. But just because it's easy to change things doesn't always mean it's the right time or situation to do so. This is where Progressive Delivery shines—by providing a framework that balances capability with responsibility, speed with sustainability.

In physics, understanding jerk helps engineers design better systems—from elevator controls to autonomous vehicles. Similarly, understanding the forces of technological change through Progressive Delivery helps us build better software systems that respect both the need for rapid innovation and users' capacity to adapt to change. Modern software delivery works because we have an abundance of software and network resources, the autonomy to find the best path to solve a problem, the alignment to work within a distributed system, and the automation to preserve our energy for novel and challenging tasks. Through Progressive Delivery, we can ensure that this malleability serves both the creators and consumers of technology, making change not just possible but purposeful.

Chapter 2

ABUNDANCE

If quantity forms the goals of our feedback loops, if quantity is the center of our attention and language and institutions, if we motivate ourselves, rate ourselves, and reward ourselves on our ability to produce quantity, then quantity will be the result. You can look around and make up your own mind about whether quantity or quality is the outstanding characteristic of the world in which you live.

—**Donella H. Meadows,** *Thinking in Systems: A Primer*

In physics, potential energy is the energy that is stored in a system. As we have explained, jerk is the sudden, unexpected change in acceleration that throws us off balance. Abundance, for developers and builders of software, is how many resources you have available—technological potential energy. This potential energy powers your innovation. When used responsibly, abundance can provide steady acceleration and help avoid the jerk caused by exposing too much change too quickly to your users.

Over the past fifty years or so, our society has moved from an environment where technology was a scarce resource to one of abundance, where technology is not only cheap but all-pervasive. This transition represents a fundamental shift in the world of software development—from a world of constrained motion to one of technological momentum.

Prices of memory, compute, and storage continue to drop as maximum densities continue to climb. We're all familiar with Moore's Law, first described by Gordon Moore, Intel's cofounder, in 1965. He predicted that the number of transistors on a single computer chip would double roughly every two years with a negligible increase in cost.[1] This exponential growth creates a form of technological inertia—a mass and velocity that, once in motion, becomes difficult to slow down or redirect. Though this initial observation was in relation to compute, the same growth of density has been roughly equivalent for both memory and storage as well.

At the time of this writing, a 1-terabyte hard drive costs less than $30. Phones are considerably more powerful than mainframes were twenty years ago. The cloud made, and continues to make, this abundance accessible to anyone with a credit card. High-speed networking and 5G have removed bandwidth as a limitation in most regions. Software, too, is cheap. (Or even free, as in a puppy, which may have no up-front cost but a lot of maintenance expenses.) Open source has driven an abundance revolution in software. Each of these developments adds mass to the technological momentum that organizations must now harness rather than resist.

So, what does all this abundance mean in the context of Progressive Delivery? And how can we harness this momentum without creating disruptive jerks in our systems and for our users? Let's define it clearly:

a·bun·dance (/ə'bənd(ə)ns/): More than enough of all the resources required to accomplish a task.

In the context of Progressive Delivery, abundance (along with autonomy) forms the foundation of a better developer experience, much like the electrical grid supports our modern life. This translates to better product management and applications and services that users can adopt at their own pace. It is part of the foundation that absorbs the shock of rapid change.

Historical Context of Abundance

Historically, software delivery was defined by resource constraints—a world of low technological mass and high friction. Like trying to push a heavy object across a rough surface, every movement requires significant force. Waterfall methodologies were partly a response to this lack of resources. You had to get things right (in theory, at least) the first time, with specifications and infrastructure requirements defined up front.

In this constrained environment, change was expensive and jerky— each new project represented a major acceleration from a standing start.

(Another way to look at this is if you graph innovation, waterfall is a step function, Agile made the steps smaller, and continuous delivery allowed the steps to smooth out to a curve.) Teams were split into different functional groups, each with their own infrastructure—developers needed access to development servers; test and QA had their own servers, storage, and so on; and production was a separate team with its own infrastructure and tools. High availability incurred huge costs—each extra "9" of availability added an order of magnitude to system cost. There was a great deal of replication and a lot of time spent waiting for permission. A development team could wait literally months to have resources provisioned to start a new project or application, creating a stop-start motion full of technological jerks.

The Abundance Transition

Think of the abundance transition we've made since 1995, when the internet revolution kicked into gear. In the late 1990s, a growing startup would need to raise literally millions of dollars simply to operate at scale, including funding for databases, application servers, testing, storage, networking gear, and marketing. At the time, hiring and staffing weren't the major costs; infrastructure was. Even developer tools were a significant expense, costing hundreds if not thousands of dollars. The Eclipse project—a free, open-source IDE—wasn't launched until 2001. Mercury Interactive was charging customers hundreds of thousands of dollars for licenses to use its testing products for e-commerce applications. Infrastructure abundance enabled and required a change in working practices.

The Agile Manifesto was published in 2001, but the concepts introduced in that movement became widely adopted as the cloud took off.

Individuals and interactions over processes and tools
Working software over comprehensive documentation
Customer collaboration over contract negotiation
Responding to change over following a plan
That is, while there is value in the items on the right, we value the items on the left more.[2]

All of this comes from an abundance mindset. When Jez Humble and David Farley introduced the concept of deployment pipelines in *Continuous Delivery*, published in 2010, the cloud was just taking off.[3] In the intervening years, abundance has supercharged those practices.

In 2005, Daniel Terhorst-North and Jez Humble introduced the idea of blue-green deployments as a response to a client having significantly different test and production environments.[4] They wanted to be able to smoke test in one environment, the "shadow," which replicated production, before moving workloads over. This approach came from an abundance mindset and is now a common practice thanks to cloud abundance and automation capabilities. The cloud doesn't just enable abundance; it does so with powerful automation built in.

Abundance and automation enable Progressive Delivery by providing new ways of working.

Virtualization, Abundance, and Cloud Computing

The mainstream availability of virtualization was another jerk for software developers. While virtualization was initially positioned for IT efficiency, driving greater resource utilization, it also underpinned a new approach to resource availability. The same server could be used for development, test, QA, or production, so separate teams were not fighting over scarce resources. Organizations also began to collapse functional silos. Plus, sophisticated automation meant environments could be treated as ephemeral rather than built for (long-term) purpose. Automation enabled abundance.

This trend accelerated and expanded with the emergence of cloud computing. While the cloud was originally composed of virtual machines, we now also use container-based architectures, enabling ever-greater granularity of compute resources.

As resources became more abundant, the ability to incorporate software into everything became more economical. The cost of developing more value and delivering it to users dropped precipitously. A single individual can build and deploy an application. That autonomy and agency are now a baseline expectation for software, not an exception. What became more important was understanding user needs and figuring out how to meet them in a commercially viable way.

What About On-Prem?

The cloud is an exemplar of digital abundance, but sometimes costs are hidden. Many organizations are currently considering repatriating some workloads because they are concerned with performance or the spiraling costs of cloud hosting.

When we consider abundance in the context of Progressive Delivery, two critical factors emerge: First, simplified management is a form of abundance. The cloud doesn't just mean more infrastructure, but more managed services as well. If developers don't have to worry about how to manage databases, then they have more choice and capability available to focus on the way they are adding business value.

Second, the evidence indicates that cloud infrastructure provides the optimal environment for Progressive Delivery. The cloud is the key underpinning for abundance, autonomy, and automation. No other platform comes close.

Though organizations can implement Progressive Delivery patterns and practices using on-premises infrastructure, the cloud—as delivered by hyperscalers such as AWS, Microsoft Azure, and Google Cloud—is the most flexible environment for software delivery. In terms of automation capability, network routing, and the flexibility to clone and fork infrastructure, the cloud is more flexible than on-premises.

For organizations with on-premises requirements, Kubernetes and container-based infrastructures provide a viable alternative (they're called "cloud native" for a reason). While it's certainly possible to implement Progressive Delivery patterns using these technologies alongside modern automation tools like Ansible and HashiCorp Terraform, the effort is substantial. Platform engineering teams must build and maintain much of what cloud providers deliver as managed services. This additional work—creating infrastructure, managing scaling, implementing security—represents significant overhead that detracts from focusing on customer value.

The willingness to embrace cloud services stands as a strong indicator of an organization's commitment to abundance thinking. It signals a prioritization of developer productivity and innovation speed over traditional infrastructure control patterns. Even in organizations that have physical or security constraints, virtualized systems and containers allow for more flexibility outside of a capital-expenditure budget.

There will always be outliers, and if your business is operating physical infrastructure at the scale of a public cloud provider, your teams will definitely benefit from the same Progressive Delivery practices.

Key Principles and Applications

In physics, potential energy becomes useful only when it's transformed into kinetic energy, ideally with a controlled, reliable flow. Abundance transforms the physics of software delivery in much the same way that modern electrical grids transformed society. It's not merely about generating more power; it's about fundamentally changing how that power is distributed, regulated, and used.

Abundance includes tangible resources like compute, storage, and bandwidth, but its true power comes from the transformative shift in mindset from "Why do you need that?" to "Is there any reason you shouldn't have that?" This represents a profound rebalancing of forces in the system. Just as an electrical grid with sophisticated transformers and load balancers can maintain steady power through demand spikes without brownouts, organizations with abundance thinking can absorb the jerks of rapid innovation without disrupting their forward momentum.

In the resource-scarce past, restricting access made economic sense. Like power rationing during shortages, the friction of approval processes protected valuable assets. Today, however, the cost of testing often exceeds the cost of the resources themselves. When a "test machine" represented hardware worth more than a developer's weekly compensation plus dedicated internal support, careful gatekeeping was justified. Now, when the same capability might represent just $0.73 of a multi-thousand-dollar cloud invoice, the friction of approval creates unnecessary resistance, like forcing users to file paperwork before turning on a light switch.

The following principles exemplify how abundance thinking transforms the physics of software delivery, creating a reliable power grid of innovation that delivers consistent value while smoothing out potentially disruptive technological jerks.

From Getting to Using

When resources are scarce, organizations expend enormous energy simply acquiring what they need—the "getting" phase consumes attention, budget, and time. Abundance fundamentally shifts this equation. Sufficiency lets us change our focus from *getting* to *using*—from acquiring infrastructure to creating value with it. It's the difference between struggling to generate enough electricity and being able to focus on what you can build with reliable power.

As technology matures, it changes from an end in itself to a way to get things done. We shouldn't think about infrastructure itself, but rather how to use it to build an app that delivers value to users. The existence of new abundance, like the cloud, puts this kind of thinking into stark relief.

AWS talks about avoiding undifferentiated heavy lifting as a core principle. From the *AWS Well-Architected Framework*:

> *Stop spending money on undifferentiated heavy lifting: AWS does the heavy lifting of data center operations like racking, stacking, and powering servers. It also removes the operational burden of managing operating systems and applications with managed services. This permits you to focus on your customers and business projects rather than on IT infrastructure.[5]*

We don't need to *get* information technology (IT) because IT is all around us. The question is how we use IT to get from A to B to C, how we make progress in delivering applications and services. "Getting" is undifferentiated heavy lifting. "Using" is creating new services and new value for customers.

Abundance and Alignment: Giving the User Options

In our equation of how the four A's balance, we use alignment (along with automation) to constrain abundance and autonomy from runaway growth. This is intended to help teams avoid building beyond the needs of the users and delivering features that never get used. Progressive Delivery can also include putting the user in charge of when they choose to adopt a new service. IT creates options alongside product management, but the user decides when to adopt them.

Just as modern electrical systems offer user-controlled switches rather than centrally regulated power, Progressive Delivery separates the availability of features from their activation. Imagine if the power company controlled the dimmer switch in your living room. Instead, we generate and transmit the capability, but users control when to flip the switch.

For example, software developers can use a blue-green deployment to test new services before moving all customers over to them. This capability also enables product teams to strategically roll out features to different user segments. Smart organizations today increasingly allow users to decide when they start using a service or feature.

Google introduced Gmail Labs on June 5, 2008—an option in Gmail that allowed users to test new features and provide feedback to Google. This was a fundamental step forward in cloud-based product management.

More recently, Microsoft has adopted similar approaches. Outlook, for example, now has a "Try the new Outlook" toggle in the upper-right corner of the classic Outlook window. Here, the user is firmly in charge of when and how they adopt a set of new features. This is a great example of modern Progressive Delivery practices.

With Atlassian, for some new features (like new boards and issue transitions), users can opt into the new experience (and give feedback) or stay in the classic mode for a period of time. Atlassian did a great job of transitioning users from the old issues editor to the new using Progressive Delivery patterns, including phased rollouts and extensive user feedback.

The good news? These same experimental patterns pioneered by major corporations are accessible to everyone. What once required massive engineering investments has become standardized practice, with powerful platforms making implementation straightforward. The automation infrastructure has evolved dramatically, transforming capabilities that teams once had to build from scratch. Feature flagging systems, for instance, have gone from custom-built solutions to robust, off-the-shelf products with thriving ecosystems.

We can all take advantage of abundance.

The bad news? Today, many of us still force updates on users that annoy them at best and, at worst, break the core experience entirely. In January 2025, Sonos CEO Patrick Spence was forced to resign after an app update in 2024 broke core user workflows, such as sleep timers, adding songs to a queue, and managing WiFi connectivity.[6] Users were rightly furious, responding to a fundamental misalignment between the brand and the market.

While it's clear we should use feature flags and give users options, abundance goes even further. With abundant resources, running two service versions simultaneously becomes a real possibility. You can maintain the current version for mainstream users while offering the next version to early adopters and supporting the legacy version for those who aren't ready to migrate.

This transforms Progressive Delivery into a strategic service management approach. We gain the power to be deliberate about managing technical debt, gracefully sunsetting outdated features rather than abruptly removing them. These decisions shift from a purely technical concern to a business alignment question.

At its core, Progressive Delivery puts users in control of their experience. When users complain about forced updates, they're often expressing frustration at their lack of agency. By giving them a choice in when and how they adopt changes, we create happier users and opportunities for new business models built on flexible, user-driven rollouts.

Abundance, Elasticity, and Optionality

In a world of digital abundance, we ask questions that embrace a variety of possibilities and users. We've moved from simple motion to complex adaptive systems that can absorb and dampen technological jerks. Thus, we can build with customization and optionality in mind, understanding that resources are not universal, and users may indeed be resource constrained.

Abundance creates technological shock absorbers—we expect spikes in usage but also work to optimize and harmonize workloads when we see that work focus has shifted. We sometimes shut things down because abundance is most effective when we can clearly distinguish between what drives us toward our goals and what no longer delivers value. This adaptability allows our systems to maintain steady momentum even when faced with external forces trying to jerk them in different directions.

In an abundance world, we don't need to choose between A and B; instead, we can test an entire range of possible outcomes or options simultaneously. In a world with elastic response to demand, you don't need to own a whole datacenter to handle the spike in traffic from the Super Bowl. Instead, you can rent that capacity from a content delivery network (CDN) as you need it, both around predictable and unpredictable events.

Elastic scale serves in both building and operating software. During development, it enables thorough testing with production-like loads—a capability previously unimaginable for most organizations. Consider the challenge of stress-testing a major system. How do you create a production replica of a major production system and then generate a huge amount of load across it? With cloud abundance, you can spin up environments on demand without massive capital investment.

An abundant software world isn't just about raw capacity and volume— it's directed capacity. Like an electrical grid that doesn't just generate power but delivers it precisely where and when needed, abundance provides both the resources and the frameworks to guide their use. Opinionated guidance and well-established patterns give teams confidence when doing novel or unusual things, ensuring they are heading in the right direction.

Recognizing Abundance Constraints

Despite this progress and abundance, not all organizations have a true abundance mindset. You can spot this by examining how decisions are made in your environment. When teams must justify small experiments, when accessibility features are dismissed as "too expensive," or when time tracking becomes more important than user outcomes, these are symptoms of scarcity thinking, not an abundance mindset.

The most telling example is in how your organization responds to new ideas. If the immediate reaction is "Can we do that? Is it allowed?" then you're likely operating without an abundance mindset. Other signs of low abundance might include:

- a heavy process burden in requesting additional resources
- exaggerated organizational fear of (small) failure
- resistance to any change because of potential costs
- zero-sum thinking—"If that person gets more, I will get less."

If you are in an organization with abundance constraints, do what you can to create local abundance. If the organization is too resistant to creating abundance, they are probably not organizationally prepared to work toward Progressive Delivery.

Abundance Is Additive

Another aspect of software abundance is that we all stand on the shoulders of giants. As software developers, we depend on languages, packages, libraries, and other dependencies that have been written by others. It doesn't make sense to write our own stacks, from the machine code on up, when the software is available to us at our fingertips. In fact, few of us write compilers or new programming languages.

At every level of software, we are building on the work of others, and we benefit from the abundance of this work. Because we can use the work and standards of others, our software fits with other software, and we don't have to re-create it. Like the modern electrical grid, we don't generate our own power or build transformers from scratch; we simply connect to standardized outlets, focusing our energy on what we'll do with that power.

Consider a typical web application today: It might use React for the front end (created by Facebook), run on Node.js (developed by Joyent), store data in MongoDB (from MongoDB Inc.), authenticate users with Auth0 (by Okta), process payments via Stripe, and deploy automatically through GitHub Actions. Each component represents thousands of engineering hours that the development team doesn't need to replicate. Abundance means there is almost always code at hand for solved problems, which means we are free to work on unsolved problems—the unique value our application provides to users.

AI is accelerating this abundance dramatically. Generative AI (GenAI) is itself based on abundance. Large language models (LLMs) were trained on vast datasets, and now they're generating code on behalf of developers. AI is not just finding software to build solutions with; it's generating the solutions themselves. Some people flinch away from the thought of having so many dependencies on other teams and companies—and indeed LLMs—but we already exist in a mesh of dependencies

This abundance also creates challenges, such as the danger of potential vulnerabilities in third-party libraries. But Progressive Delivery allows security testing to be added to our pipelines before deployment and again before rollout. It's another layer of security. Management of dependencies is a key aspect of modern software testing, and Progressive Delivery maps to it quite well.

Benefits of Abundance

Engineering teams once had limited access to the software they needed to build and deploy new services and applications. This software is now effectively free, available on GitHub and other repositories, with marginal costs of zero. This transition is akin to moving from a system with high friction and little mass to one with low friction and increasing mass, resulting in significant momentum. Once set in motion, development becomes harder to stop than to continue.

Distributed version control systems have removed developer dependence on central repositories, again enabling abundance. The availability of managed services means we're not even constrained by the cost of managing infrastructure. Cloud resource limitations are effectively a thing of the past—unless you count cost. This abundance has enabled entirely new ways of working—a fundamental change in the physics of development that transformed jerky stop-start motion into smooth continuous delivery.

We can measure abundance both quantitatively and qualitatively. A quantitative measurement would be how long it takes to go from request to allocation for a particular resource. What resources are available to developers and developer teams? A qualitative measurement uses surveys and interviews to ask developers if they have the resources they need to accomplish their tasks.

Today, Apple sets the bar for local machine performance. A common proxy for abundance is the availability of recent model MacBook Pros. (If your developers can't use the machines they want for work, then abundance may be in question.) Of course, some developers and organizations prefer Windows, and that's totally fine. In that case, can a developer get the latest AMD or Intel processors, or even ARM-based machines, and all the RAM they desire?

Abundance within boundaries does not mean abundance without constraints. You can't build anything without understanding constraints and making trade-offs. These constraints are often expressed as costs, but the classic aphorism "Good. Cheap. Fast. Pick two." is another expression of constraints. Time is inelastic, and there are some things we can't just pay to speed up—some jerks in the system cannot be entirely eliminated, only managed.

But abundance frees software developers to do their best work. It removes the need to wait for permission. Organizations should get out of the way, where possible, and allow builders to build.

This tension between the concept of instantly responsive software and the time, effort, resources, and underlying physical systems that support it is the core of Progressive Delivery's problem. What is meaningful to deliver? What adds value? What supports the other parts of the structure? What do we need to change and streamline to iteratively improve the act of delivering and the experience of receiving?

Abundance enabled a Cambrian explosion that has changed how we think about software and product delivery. Organizations don't have a single integrated monolithic technology stack and may not even have a central technology administration. Instead, different parts of the organization solve the problem at hand that is closest to them, without needing to ask for permission. Abundance enables autonomy and radical delegation.

Challenges and Considerations of Abundance

Abundance can come with its own problems. When something is cheap, we tend to value it less. Abundance can also lead to problems of scale in disposal and management. Abundance creates its own form of inertia—objects in motion tend to stay in motion, even when that motion is no longer serving our goals. Just as a heavy vehicle with momentum requires more sophisticated braking systems, our systems of abundance require more sophisticated governance to prevent runaway acceleration.

Abundance can lead to carelessness in how we use resources. In the boom times, when resources are cheap, we don't meter them. Then, when resources are more constrained, we don't have the systems to use them efficiently. People raised in well-watered areas do not build the habits of water conservation that people raised in drought areas do. In a ZIRP software boom, there is little incentive to cap spending on resources since the focus is on growth.

Without proper control systems, the technological momentum we've built can cause destructive jerks as competing forces pull in different directions. Abundance is great, but it comes at a cost, even if the costs seem lower. For example, what will it cost to move or transfer your data from one vendor to another? Will your abundance prove illusory in the future when your development or deployment stack changes?

An organization that doesn't track cloud spending allows users to take advantage of digital abundance but is wasting money that could be better spent. Abundance and autonomy can lead to runaway spending. The cloud, for example, which began as a phenomenon driven by individuals with credit cards, is now a trillion-dollar industry. It has even spawned a FinOps foundation to help organizations spend wisely in abundance settings. FinOps being:

> *an operational framework and cultural practice which maximizes the business value of cloud, enables timely data-driven decision making, and creates financial accountability through collaboration between engineering, finance, and business teams.*[7]

While we're not going to delve deeply into cost management here—there are many other great books on the subject—it's worth noting how the organization talks about its role.

> *FinOps is all about removing blockers; empowering engineering teams to deliver better features, apps, and migrations faster; and enabling a cross-functional conversation about where to invest and when. Sometimes a business will decide to tighten the belt; sometimes it'll decide to invest more. But now teams know why they're making those decisions.*[8]

Another way to look at abundance and runaway costs is the current debate about cloud repatriation. Some now argue that running on-premises infrastructure is cheaper than using hyperscale cloud services. This idea was expressed most pithily by venture capital firm Andreessen Horowitz in a 2022 post, "The Cost of Cloud, a Trillion Dollar Paradox," which claimed: "You're crazy if you don't start in the cloud; you're crazy if you stay on it."[9]

Whether you agree with this thesis or not, it gets to the paradox of cloud abundance. Convenience can increase direct costs, so it's important to be intentional. If abundance enables Progressive Delivery, your ability to get the right product to the right customer at the right time, then that's worth investing in. In some cases, enterprises will decide these costs are not, in fact, worth it. For example, in late 2024, GEICO announced a significant cloud repatriation effort.[10]

Not all costs are monetary, such as environmental impact and access problems that are not role-based. Not everyone has the same access to the servers and bandwidth that technologists often take for granted. Just because it worked on your WiFi network doesn't mean it will work well, and at a reasonable cost, in all parts of the world. Progressive Delivery can enable you to understand differences in infrastructure ubiquity and work with them, testing in different regions and on different networks. Operating in a gracefully degraded state is an important way to make sure software is accessible to as many people as possible.

Abundance also often leads to data management problems. The instinct to "store everything" doesn't necessarily improve analysis quality and often increases cost.

Think of your data lake as an actual hydroelectric reservoir. When properly channeled, it generates tremendous power for your organization. But just like a real dam, sediment accumulates over time. Without proper management, your data lake fills with silt—outdated information, duplicate records, and irrelevant metrics—making your data lake shallower and less valuable. Just as reservoir managers must properly control flow and waste, data stewards must establish retention policies and quality controls.

The challenge is compounded because the inflow of data is only partially under our control, and its original quality varies widely. With abundance, the question shifts from "Can we store this?" to "Should we store this, and for how long?" Observability provides a clear example of the challenges of abundance. While unlimited data collection offers unprecedented insights, it comes with substantial costs, particularly when dealing with high-cardinality datasets.

High-cardinality fields—attributes like userIds or shoppingCartIds that might have hundreds of thousands of unique values—can dramatically increase storage requirements and processing overhead. When organizations complain about excessive charges from observability vendors, they're often experiencing the downside of abundance thinking: collecting everything without strategic filtering. The issue isn't necessarily the vendor's pricing model, but rather the absence of thoughtful indexing strategies or the accumulation of data that provides minimal analytical value.

Abundance made modern observability possible in the first place. It enabled the collection and analysis of logs, metrics, and system traces at a scale previously unimaginable. However, this capability shift created a new pain point where observability vendors now compete primarily on cost efficiency rather than just feature sets.

This balance between data abundance and cost management is particularly critical for Progressive Delivery. Observability provides an essential feedback loop when testing services in production through feature flags or canary deployments. Without comprehensive and queryable monitoring, teams lack the confidence to implement progressive rollout strategies.

The observability industry has responded to this tension with innovative approaches. Increasingly, observability platforms are being built on efficient open-source data lakes like ClickHouse or proprietary platforms like Snowflake. These solutions enable cost-effective querying across commodity object storage instead of relying on specialized (and expensive) time-series databases—another example of abundance driving innovation in response to its own challenges.

Getting Started with Abundance

In a world where technological jerks have become the norm—where software updates can disrupt workflows without warning, and new platforms emerge seemingly overnight—abundance offers both a challenge and a solution. The same acceleration that creates jarring experiences for users can also provide the resources to smooth these transitions.

Software now permeates nearly every aspect of our lives, from morning alarms to evening entertainment. Each interaction represents a potential moment of technological jerk—an unexpected acceleration that can either delight or disorient. Progressive Delivery helps manage these moments by leveraging abundance not just as raw computing power, but as a comprehensive approach to change management.

The abundance mindset transforms the fundamental question from "Do we have enough resources?" to "How can we best direct our virtually unlimited resources to create smooth, controlled acceleration rather than jarring jerks?" As we build software, we need to think past pure capacity and bring in the wisdom to build in ways that respect users' need for stability amid innovation—that is, how to build the right thing for the right people at the right time.

Evaluating for Abundance

As you begin to look at your software development practices through the lens of Progressive Delivery, understanding abundance is important. What *does* abundance mean in your organization?

Here are some questions to consider as you evaluate and work to better understand what abundance means for your team:

- What is the most constraining factor in your environment?
- How much time does it take to provision a resource?
- What is the cost of doing something in time, worked hours, or money? How often is this activity performed per day/week? By how many people?
- How do you handle excess capacity?
- If you had infinite capacity in one place, where would you put it?
- What do you rely on that is mission-critical?
- What is your fail-safe mode? If something goes wrong, what happens?
- What are your core dependencies? Which are homegrown versus outsourced? (What do you build versus buy?)
- Do you offer developers choice and budget in their tooling, and do you have constraints on the interoperability of their choices?
- Do you encourage developers to use AI tools, and do you provide a budget accordingly?

- What is the abundance you are building versus the abundance you're renting?
- Is there a way to prune things automatically without repeated human cognitive cost?
- How would you deliver to a mobile app that doesn't always have internet? (Abundance is not always universal.)
- Are you limited by what you can do or what it would cost to do it?

Tools and Processes That Enable Abundance

Many organizations use the following tools and patterns to help them successfully manage abundance. For those interested in furthering their practices, here are some to consider:

- cloud-native computing
- elastic scaling
- open-source software
- observability
- release progression
- testing in production
- blue-green deployments
- A/B testing and experimentation

While this list is by no means exhaustive, it is a starting place to explore as you consider what abundance means for you. Furthermore, not all of these will necessarily solve every use case. Rather, it's important to evaluate your needs using the list of questions we shared earlier. From there, you can begin to explore what tools and practices will support you in your efforts.

Conclusion

It's important to remember that abundance through the lens of Progressive Delivery is not using everything all at once. It is accurately understanding specific needs and building for those needs. Abundance is not just capacity and volume; it's the ability for capacity and volume to be well-directed. This is alignment on the builder/developer side of the equation. We have chosen to incorporate this into abundance since this type of alignment is more about the resources used to build a company, and not about the software being delivered to users.

Just as a skilled driver harnesses the momentum of a vehicle to navigate smoothly without jarring accelerations or jerky stops, Progressive Delivery harnesses the inertia of technological abundance to deliver change in a way that users can absorb. It transforms the potentially disruptive force of rapid technological change into a smooth, controlled acceleration that propels organizations forward without throwing their users off balance. In a world where technological jerk has become commonplace, abundance, properly managed, becomes a stabilizing force that allows us to move quickly without losing our traction.

Now that we've explored the concept of abundance in Progressive Delivery, let's explore a case study that illustrates these principles in practice. We'll see how abundance, generally, and the cloud, specifically, enabled software organizations to do things that were not possible before.

Chapter 3
CASE STUDY: SUMO LOGIC

Sumo Logic is a great example of a company built as cloud-enabled abundance arrived on the market, which influenced all of their decision-making and architectural approaches. It was founded in 2010 by a team with experience in log management, big data, and security. They set out to create a cloud-first software-as-a-service (SaaS) log analytics company, built on AWS and designed to monitor events generated by cloud-based services.

Cloud-based monitoring is different from traditional on-premises approaches because you don't have direct access to hardware metrics, because, for example, the servers are running in the cloud. APIs, however, are publishing huge amounts of data about system and application performance. In this example, data became the problem rather than instrumentation, so the company focused squarely on data management. Data volumes led to an abundance mindset, which also played into the company becoming an advanced Progressive Delivery case study.

Sumo Logic was acquired by Francisco Partners in a private equity transaction valued at $1.7 billion in February 2023. By then, it had carved out a solid position as a leader in cloud-based log management.

Situation

The first AWS primitives arrived in 2006. Launched in 2010, Sumo Logic was in a position to build an architecture from scratch on top of AWS, which was swiftly maturing. Sumo Logic used its own product to provide observ-ability, enabling feedback loops as it built, tested, and deployed new services.

This timing is significant in the context of abundance. As discussed in Chapter 2, the software industry has been shifting from a scarcity mindset to an abundance mindset since the late 1990s. Sumo Logic emerged at a perfect moment to take full advantage of the abundance the cloud provided, without the legacy constraints that hampered established enterprises.

AWS was a capable platform, but Sumo Logic still had to build a lot of its own infrastructure. For example, it built its own feature flag system and even its own infrastructure-as-code provisioning system. So, while it was building a very sophisticated automated infrastructure for building, testing, and deploying the platform, it was also incurring a fair amount of technical debt. This represents the "getting to using" transition description in Chapter 2. Building their own tools was still necessary, but they were focusing on how to use infrastructure rather than simply acquiring it.

There were several key architectural decisions at Sumo Logic that enabled Progressive Delivery and testing in production, including:

- Adopting a service-oriented architecture (SOA) approach, with loosely coupled services that could be updated and scaled independently. This provided flexibility for progressive rollouts.
- Implementing feature flags and shadow deployments to test changes in production without impacting all customers. This allowed Sumo Logic to experiment and validate changes before full rollouts.
- Focusing on observability and cost optimization to understand the impact of changes and manage the costs of the cloud infrastructure.

These decisions directly embody the key principles and applications of abundance. The SOA approach means different services can scale and be tested independently while also allowing multiple versions of a service to run simultaneously. Sumo Logic practices canary deployment and then looks at what sort of customers choose to use the new feature. This practice is made possible by their extensive use of feature flags.

As Bruno Kurtic, cofounder of Sumo Logic, told us: "We roll out a new service to 5% of our customers first. What sort of users choose to use this feature? We roll out the service then leverage our logs to understand the behaviors of the system and users. Logs are integral to understanding how new code is being shipped, how you do A/B testing in production. We do testing in production."

Finally, Sumo Logic's observability focus means it is constantly using feedback loops, understanding user behaviors, and adjusting system behavior accordingly. A key lesson here is that logs are integral to understanding how new code is being shipped and can underpin A/B testing in production, aligning the needs of users, developers, and product owners. Sumo Logic's approach, and focus on optionality and observability, underpinned by the abundance of system resources, enables them to align releases with actual user needs and behaviors.

Giving Developers Their Own Production Infrastructure

One of the best examples of cloud-enabled abundance at Sumo Logic was how it provided images to developers. Technical leadership wanted to avoid "But it worked on my machine." finger-pointing between operations and developers, so the development environment had to be as close to production as possible. Therefore, Sumo Logic built a minimal layer for "personal deployments" on AWS that allowed developers to easily test their code in what was effectively a production environment, including all of the microservices—a "mini-Sumo."

This approach perfectly embodies "from getting to using." In the pre-abundance era, developers would have spent significant time acquiring and configuring test environments or working in test environments that did not closely mimic production. At Sumo Logic, they could work in an environment that was as close to production as possible.

Cloud abundance represents a dramatic transformation from the historical context, where development, test, QA, and production teams were split into functional silos, each with their own infrastructure, and developers had local machines that didn't replicate these infrastructures at all.

This streamlined development environment greatly improved the developer experience and the ability to test changes. This abundance also empowered autonomy, allowing any developer to spin up a full Sumo Logic stack, ideally just for an hour or so.

However, giving all developers their own Sumo Logic could get expensive quickly if developers didn't turn these instances off. After all, abundance needs to be ephemeral to be cost-effective. At first, it was about reminding developers to turn these mini-Sumos off, but naturally, the company soon built a set of scripts, which became an internal app, to go out and kill clusters that weren't being used. They called it Reaper.

Autonomy driven by abundance is great, but automation was needed to keep things under control, enabling alignment between the needs of the engineer, the platform owner, and the CFO.

Cloud Bursts and Feature Optionality

Another facet of the need to maintain alignment between the business and the availability of resources is consumption-based scaling. Sumo Logic was architected to scale elastically, taking advantage of cloud resources as its customers' workloads grew. The cloud allows organizations to take advantage of hyperscaler abundance, even for customers that are extremely "bursty" from a workload perspective, such as online gaming companies. Think of the growth of Pokémon GO or Fortnite. Load testing should replicate this kind of workload fluctuation, where customers might create so much extra traffic that they effectively create a distributed denial of service (DDoS) traffic pattern by accident. But even with load testing, a truly unexpected success can drive resource utilization well above expectations.

Sumo Logic built feature optionality into its core architecture. In order to handle system load, Sumo Logic can turn any feature in its platform on or off. The company can also turn any feature in its platform on and roll it out to one specific customer in a particular region for a particular use case to test it before wider deployment. Here the cloud advantage underpinning Progressive Delivery is about easy access to sophisticated networking, which is a form of abundance in its own right.

Progressive Delivery for Machine Learning

Driven by infrastructure abundance, Sumo Logic can conduct shadow tests of new machine learning models in production, something that would have been unthinkable in the pre-cloud era.

For example, a customer might complain that Sumo Logic's pattern recognition wasn't working. The danger here is that if the company changes the algorithm for other customers, it might break their experience. Therefore, Sumo Logic needed to silently spin up a couple of clusters and test the algorithm's performance.

Sumo Logic does candidate testing of each service it rolls out. To do this, they have a shadow copy of Sumo Logic that is used for testing, industry regulations, and so on. The entire infrastructure is replicated—this is literally testing in production, driven by abundance.

The clone was deployed in a different datacenter with a different set of engineers, which also created some interesting management overheads. This full system replication exemplifies the technological inertia we discussed in Chapter 2—the ability to build momentum and stability through abundance. By maintaining parallel systems, Sumo Logic creates a counterbalance to technological jerk, absorbing changes rather than being disrupted by them.

Complications

Abundance led to sprawl being a key issue, alongside technical debt. Thus, Sumo Logic made extensive use of feature flags. Over time, however, there were so many feature flags that the entire system became unwieldy. What began as a mechanism enabling flexibility became an issue for engineering. The Sumo Logic team ended up rewriting the feature flag system to make it better adapted to modern software engineering practices with version control and a Git-based workflow. Today, they would likely choose a packaged third-party feature flag solution. Not all abundance arrives at once, and any startup incurs technical debt.

By 2015, it was clear Sumo Logic needed to reduce infrastructure costs overall. So, it spun up a group, which included a data scientist, tasked with reducing infrastructure costs, and called them the Prosperity Team. This effort was a dramatic success, increasing margins for cost to serve from around 30% to over 70%.

Abundance always needs to be managed. You need to be intentional, or costs get out of control. The question becomes how to maintain cost controls and avoid sprawl while allowing abundance to underpin alignment with the business goals of a fast-growing startup.

Question

It's currently commonplace to say that every company is a software company. But if that's the case, there is a whole set of practices associated with being a software company that are really tough: managing open-source infrastructure at scale, or dealing with software dependencies, or keeping current with common vulnerabilities and exposures (CVEs). We all get blamed for poor customer experiences—software companies certainly do. But in terms of managing your own estate and identifying what is actually a competitive advantage, that's a thorny set of engineering questions with no simple set of answers.

As Christian Beedgen, one of Sumo Logic's founders, put it during an interview with James Governor in February of 2025,

> Our declarative deployment system was a competitive advantage...until it wasn't. Because it was bespoke, and we had to maintain it. Over time Sumo Logic hired new people with a different set of expectations about industry standard infrastructure, such as HashiCorp or LaunchDarkly. These folks also had skills using these platforms. So, abundance, in the case of venture capital, meant Sumo Logic could do some incredible core engineering work.

But it is possible to over-engineer things, and managing technical debt is always hard.[1]

Beedgen's observation highlights the transition Sumo Logic made from building its own provisioning and feature flagging management tools to adopting industry standards. This illustrates both the benefits of abundance and the challenges of maintaining bespoke solutions in an ecosystem increasingly built on shared platforms.

Summary: Abundance as the Organizational Forcing Factor

Abundance is a powerful forcing factor enabling new organizational practices, working methods, and workflows in tech. Two of the main beneficiaries of digital abundance are the developer and the engineering organization because of the autonomy it gives them. Abundance removes the need to ask for permission, removes bottlenecks, and allows engineers to get on with their work—no more time waiting for infrastructure to be provisioned. Of course, greater autonomy requires new management approaches to enable alignment, which we'll explore in upcoming chapters.

Sumo Logic exemplifies this transformation. Their "mini-Sumo" environments eliminated wait times for developers. Their elastic architecture removed the permission bottlenecks for scaling. Their shadow deployment capabilities allowed for testing without traditional approval gates. Each of these innovations demonstrates how abundance transformed the physics of their software delivery, from the jerky stop-start motion of the scarcity era to the smooth Progressive Delivery enabled by abundance.

Autonomy, derived from abundance, allows organizations to move faster, ship more products, and roll out new services more quickly. It also reduces the likelihood of burnout, by increasing agency for developers and users. This radical delegation, as explained more in future chapters, is a fundamental improvement in working culture.

The Sumo Logic case study provides a concrete example of both the possibilities and challenges of abundance as a foundational pillar of Progressive Delivery. Their journey from founding in 2010 to acquisition in 2023 spans the maturation of cloud abundance, demonstrating how organizations can harness technological inertia to create momentum while developing the necessary controls to prevent the destructive jerks of unmanaged acceleration.

Chapter 4

AUTONOMY

How does one reconcile autonomy, agency, responsibility, and mutuality?
What's mine to carry, what's someone else's to carry, and what do we hold
collectively?

—**Mia Birdsong**, *How We Show Up: Reclaiming Family,*
Friendship, and Community

When we discussed jerk as the rate of change in acceleration, we explored
how sudden changes create instability. If abundance is the technological
potential energy—the stored energy in the system—then autonomy represents
the force vectors of your motion. Each developer (or development
team) has the ability to move things in a certain direction with the force of
their skills. When these force vectors are tightly coupled—like the cars of
a train—the direction is perfectly aligned, but the speed is limited to that
of the slowest car. When these force vectors are loosely coupled—like cars
on a freeway—the overall speed is faster and the ability to course correct
is greater.

Autonomy is about people making decisions on their own, based on
the objectives of their project or task. After all, if you can't actually use
resources as you need to, then what good are they to you?

Progressive Delivery enables us to manage change. Where abundance
gives us access to what we need to make those changes, autonomy is having
the power to make timely, relevant, and appropriate actions. Autonomy is
feeling confident that you are making a good choice based on real information
and knowing you likely won't even have to defend it. Autonomy is
being able to take actions without context switching or friction.

au·ton·o·my (/ôˈtänəmē/): The ability for an individual to act
independently from others.

When developing software, this independence means access to all necessary resources to complete a desired task. Resources can be physical or the logical aspects we mentioned in the chapter on abundance, as well as the permissions or ability to use shared services or applications without having to wait. Autonomy is the second of the two pillars of proliferation. Just like abundance, autonomy is all about the developer experience.

In order to have a Progressive Delivery environment, developers (and most creatives) need to be able to innovate and build at their own pace. Constraints on the system should be additive and intentional, not arbitrary or accidental. This requires that the deployment of software (code, apps, or services) be completely separated from the release (visibility or impact) of any changes to the end users. Without this separation of deployment and release, autonomy is not possible.

To measure autonomy quantitatively, we can track how frequently teams are "blocked" or waiting for work to be done by others. During some stages of growth or product expansion, the rate of blocking may naturally rise. During these times, it is important to invest in the tools, architecture, and resources to restore autonomy and enable future capability.

A common example is when a new product or project is starting from scratch. Like the building of a new bridge, the person who paints the lines on the road will be blocked until the road is in place. That said, as a team or company grows, resources can be allocated to projects or products as the ability to contribute emerges. Compare this to bridge maintenance or repair work, where greater autonomy can be achieved between the people repainting lines and those replacing signs. Even resurfacing the road can often be done one lane at a time, allowing utilization to continue while various work tasks occur in parallel.

Historical Context of Autonomy

Just as the abundance of computing resources evolved over time, so too has the concept of autonomy in software development. Like abundance, autonomy developed as a response to the technological jerks of traditional development models—those jarring stop-start processes that created friction and inefficiency.

Historically, software development followed a highly constrained, serialized process. Developers had to wait for their turn to work on code, progress moved in fits and starts, and the path from concept to deployment was marked by numerous jerky handoffs between specialized teams. This approach created significant friction and inertial disruption—technological jerks that impeded progress and frustrated developers and users alike.

The evolution toward greater autonomy in software development parallels the evolution toward greater abundance. As computing resources became more plentiful, development teams could move beyond the constraints of serialized processes. The results of this evolution can be seen in the progression from traditional waterfall methods to Agile development and eventually to continuous delivery.

Progressive Delivery represents the next step in this evolution, drawing from Agile and continuous delivery. While Agile optimizes for user adoption and feedback, and continuous delivery optimizes for developer autonomy and operational efficiency, Progressive Delivery looks to optimize for both. It accomplishes this by clearly separating the deployment of software to production and the release of software to users.

At some point in any software development life cycle, software needs to be deployed, or installed, on a computer to allow the code to execute and provide value. For simplicity, when we talk about deployment in this context, we are talking about deployment to the production environment.*

In Agile, software deployment and release are often treated as the same thing. Once the software is running on the computer in production, users also have access to the running code. In continuous delivery, a variety of methods are used to separate the deployment of code and the release to users. However, the motivation behind these methods is all about developer autonomy and code readiness, not user readiness and rate of adoption.

---

* We acknowledge that many organizations will have staging or pre-production environments that are used to do further validation testing. In general, this is a reasonable practice, but at some point, the code needs to be put into the production environment to be accessed by users.

This separation is crucial—it allows developers to deploy code autonomously while giving users control over their rate of change adoption. Thus, the deployment of code stays largely unchanged from the continuous delivery model, continuing to support developer autonomy. But the release of code to users requires the addition of user readiness. The goal of Progressive Delivery is to extend this choice of readiness as close to the end user of the software as appropriate.

Autonomy is directly related to the evolution and progression of the developer experience and software production. It is the ability for independent work streams to work in parallel instead of being serialized, smoothing out the jerky stop-start motion of traditional development processes and creating a more continuous and less disruptive flow of innovation. This is true for both microservice architectures and monolithic architectures. Feature flags enable code changes to happen at the right speed for development teams without affecting users or other teams.

From Git to CI/CD

When Linus Torvalds, the creator of the Linux kernel, introduced Git (a distributed source-control system for managing code with multiple contributors), he was trying to provide greater autonomy for individual developers or small teams of developers to build software in parallel. This was a critical advancement in addressing technological jerk—rather than forcing developers to wait for others or experience the jarring interruptions of code freezes, Git created a smoother developer experience. The distributed and noncommercial nature of open-source software further showed that alignment wouldn't always come from proximity or top-down management; it could also come from shared goals and agreed-upon interactions.

When looking to optimize complex systems, a common way to approach the system is to look at the flow dynamics. A frequently used example of this in software development is discussed at length in books and articles on Toyota manufacturing, including *The Toyota Way* by Jeffrey Liker.[1] The simplified principle is that in order to improve the output of a system, you need to understand where the bottlenecks form and continually look to reduce and remove bottlenecks from the system. There are two ways to do this: reduce the flow to a bottleneck (send fewer requests to a processing station) or increase the rate of processing at the bottleneck. Increasing the rate can be done one of two ways: do the processing faster or increase the number of requests that can be processed in parallel.

Prior to Git, a bottleneck for large development teams was the need to serialize the process of working on code. When working on a particular portion of code, developers would lock or restrict access to that portion of code to avoid another developer making changes that would conflict with theirs. For teams that chose to allow for parallel work, they would have to address these potential conflicts at some point or risk shipping software that was broken and unusable. This limited the speed of development and often led to long periods of limited productivity when teams would lock or "freeze" the entire code base to clean up conflicts and ensure the applications and services were able to run as intended.

With the adoption of Git, the bottleneck shifted from the contribution of code (a centralized version control system where the code was stored) to the process of getting the code from the repository to the servers (where the code would run). This meant developers could move at their own pace. They were autonomous in their ability to create code. But creating code is only part of the equation. After the code was created, it still had to be validated and tested, and it had to be run somewhere.

Figure 4.1 shows the differences in centralized and distributed version control systems. Like adding more workstations on a physical assembly line, adding more repositories reduces the bottleneck induced by having a single repository server.

As we discussed in the chapter on abundance, cloud computing and software-as-a-service (SaaS) were beginning to emerge a few years before the introduction of Git. (For the purposes of this book, we are going to focus on the delivery of software in a cloud environment instead of software that would be distributed and run locally on a physical server or computer.)

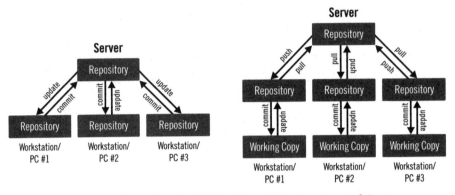

FIGURE 4.1: Centralized and Distributed Version Control Systems

Source: Adapted from Deepak Kumar Sharma, "Git | Overview | Workflow | Advantages | K21Academy," K21 Academy (blog), August 12, 2023, https://k21academy.com/devops-job-boot-camp/git-overview-workflow-advantages/.

A by-product of Git and this liberation of developer autonomy was the adoption of continuous integration (CI) and the introduction of continuous delivery (CD), which was formalized at length by Jez Humble and David Farley.[2] Developers could move more independently, and new code could be tested in an automated fashion rather than relying on manual review of known expected behavior. Continuous delivery extended the value of automation into the process of code validation (via CI) to code deployment (updating the code running on the cloud), and teams could deploy new code whenever they wanted and as frequently as they wanted.

For developers, this was amazing. They could finally optimize all parts of the process that they could touch, from code creation to the delivery of validated code to the operations team to running on cloud servers. Code was making its way to users faster than ever. To take advantage of this faster pace of deployment, teams adopted continuous integration.

Feature Flags, Toggled "On"

Feature flags are one method for separating deployment from release and increasing autonomy for developers and users. They enable the deployment of code to production without it being immediately exposed or accessible to the user.

A feature flag is a conditional or/if statement wrapped around a portion of code. The condition state is stored in a database external to the running application or service. When the computer executes the application or service and encounters the feature flag, the system retrieves the value of the feature flag from the external database and either executes the wrapped code or ignores it.

Progressive Delivery uses feature flags to provide near real-time control points in application and service code. For safety, the feature flags should be managed by a feature management platform that provides full life cycle management of flag state delivery.

While it is possible to practice Progressive Delivery without a feature management platform, we don't advise it. Release flags, operations flags, testing flags, and user-preference flags...the number of flags tends to add up quickly. Operating at scale without a robust way to track all the flags in the system is a recipe for disaster. It would be like trying to track all the changes to a code base without a code repository.

One frequently referenced example of this is the collapse of Knight Capital Group after losing $460 million in thirty minutes, due in large part to the reuse of a deprecated feature flag name. This is also a great example of why, when using feature flags, you should leverage a feature management platform to ensure visibility and consistency.[3]

Architectures with a segmented release cadence further exacerbate the need for flag life cycle tracking in the system. Modern microservice architectures enable autonomy by allowing small teams to iterate independently from one another, but they also increase the need for a high-level view of the user experience across the entire workflow, regardless of how many microservices, applications, or platforms (mobile, desktop, IoT, etc.) are involved.

Monoliths, Microservices, and APIs

Autonomy was an inevitable progression from the growing abundance of resource availability. This accelerated as new tools such as Git and feature management platforms became readily available. Along with the rise of Agile and continuous delivery, software architecture began moving from monoliths (the software as one large code repository) to microservices (multiple code repositories that are loosely coupled and can be updated or replaced independently from each other). In some cases, monolithic architecture is a very effective way to practice Progressive Delivery.

Microservice and API architecture gave teams a lot more autonomy to do whatever they felt was right within the perimeter of the microservice, as long as their API calls and responses were well-aligned with the other microservices they worked with.

The API-centric world is a great example of autonomy. Data and interfaces are openly available, and it's up to the people using them to decide what to do. There are some standards on a handful of communication protocols and some standard expectations about what every externally facing API will provide to developers.

Computers: Minions or Masters?

Historically, the autonomy granted to software users has evolved alongside technology itself. One of the key differences in how users think about technology is the "Builder Mindset" concept (inspired by *The Lego Movie*).[4] While many people very happily build Lego creations by following the kit instructions, some people see the underlying capabilities of the blocks and create double-decker couches or dinosaur cars.

Users are the same with software—some people want to understand and build with software, and some people would just like it to do what it says it will do. In early computing eras, only those with a strong Builder Mindset could effectively use technology. As interfaces evolved and simplified, systems became more accessible but often reduced user autonomy, creating technological jerks when users encountered limitations or significant changes to an interface that had been memorized instead of internalized. Today's systems increasingly try to accommodate both approaches, offering simple interfaces with progressive layers of control for those who seek it.

This historical perspective on evolving user autonomy helps explain why Progressive Delivery needs to respect different users' appetites for change and control. By understanding this evolution, we can design systems that minimize technological jerks for all users, regardless of where the builders fall on the autonomy spectrum.

From Obedient to Predictive

The historical relationship between users and computers reveals an interesting paradox in the evolution of autonomy. For much of the history of computing, we have taught that "a computer is a machine that will do exactly what you ask it to do, if you know how to ask." Calculators come up with an answer, and if the answer is wrong, the problem exists with us, in how we entered the parameters. In this era, users had clear autonomy within well-defined boundaries—you controlled what the computer did, even if wielding that control required specialized knowledge.

Gradually, in step with the growth of the internet, our relationship with computers grew more complicated. We call our interaction with software "The Algorithm," a single catch-all phrase for the ways that search, machine learning, recommendations, and customized feeds make our experience of technology unique. For many pages we visit on the internet, we are seeing an FYP (for you page), customized to our own preferences, previous searches, profile, and unknown marketing targeting indicators. We know differences exist between what we see and what another user sees and vaguely understand that they relate to our accounts, history, location, and marketing demographics. What we don't actually know, as users, is how these differences work. This shift marks a historical turning point in user autonomy, gaining convenience while sacrificing transparency and direct control.

Digital environments have stopped being straightforward and predictable and have become something that looks nondeterministic. We can influence them, but we're not always sure how to fix their behavior or even why they're doing what they're doing. This change seems to be coming faster and faster, as computers become less of a specialized work tool and more of a load-bearing pillar of our culture.

The more isolated a computer is, the more predictable it is. For most of us, the technology we interact with most often is our phone, which is always connected and giving us personalized information. Our tiny pocket computers have made us more autonomous, able to instantly access information we need to make decisions, and they have done it by making us more connected than even the most wild-haired futurists predicted.

Bringing information closer to where decisions are made is key to the modern way of conducting business. Every step that moves information further from the decision point increases the risk of misinterpretation or misinformation. Autonomy relies on not just independent actors but independent, well-informed actors who are working to accomplish similar goals.

The majority of Americans upgrade their phones every two to three years, with just over 10% upgrading every year.[5] In that time, the operating system and apps on our phones are updating and changing often. Mobile software is based on a model of push updates. This push model of updating changes what we expect from our device. Our computers are no longer just reacting to us but proactively pushing what they think we want.

Of course, this model of updates being pushed out to the user (either on our phone, the internet, or even our doorbell) is happening at an increasing rate and is more likely to make us feel the technological jerk of rapid change. This is precisely where autonomy becomes critical—giving users control over the pace of change helps absorb these technological jerks. Throughout computing history, we've oscillated between centralized and distributed models of control. Progressive Delivery represents an attempt to find a new balance that honors both developer and user autonomy.

Key Principles and Applications

Just as abundance creates technological inertia—a mass and momentum that can be difficult to redirect—autonomy gives us the ability to steer these powerful systems with precision. Rather than being at the mercy of technological jerks, autonomy transforms users from passive recipients of change into active participants who can control the pace of innovation in their lives.

Autonomy is the ability to accomplish tasks, or work, independently from others. Autonomy might touch on knowledge, process, resources, priorities, and scope of control. It's useful to think of autonomy as a property of people and teams, while automation is the way autonomy works when we delegate it to computers.

If autonomy is about people, what do they need to become autonomous? They need a locus of control, the information and context to make decisions, and the authority to make choices.

Locus of control could also be described as the actions someone has the power to take. For example, when it comes to electricity, you can turn off the breakers in your house, but not a power substation. For developers, the locus of control is usually the code they write and maintain and their method of deployment. Progressive Delivery creates more of a locus of control for users, so they can choose their update cadence and use patterns.

Making decisions is the act of balancing desired outcomes, possible risks, and context. The more knowledge and context someone has when making a decision, the more likely they are to be able to balance advantages and risks in a way that optimizes outcomes for everyone. "Delete" is a decision. "Delete from this device and the cloud platform with no option for recovery" is a decision with fuller context and information, since the decision is less reversible.

The authority to make decisions describes what someone can do independently. For a manager, this is their span of control. In military contexts, it is sometimes called an operational area. Whatever we call it, it is the extent to which someone can act without consulting others.

Once we understand that autonomy can be delegated or assumed by a person, a team, or even an organization, we can see that each level of decision-making has its own checks and balances. We'll talk more about the checks and balances in the chapter on alignment. But first, we need to discuss how we achieve the needed autonomy for our developers.

Autonomy for Developers

One example of autonomy in action is separating deployment from release. These are actually two different moments in software delivery. Deployment is when a software developer or organization puts a product or feature in the production environment. Because of the flexibility of progressive release, feature flags, and ring deployment, that product or feature may not be visible to users. Release is the moment the product or feature starts to have business value, because users can interact with it.

Think of a streaming movie. It is finished, uploaded, and cached on the streaming service's servers and mirrors—that's deployment. But until people can actually watch it, it is not released.

Autonomy enables faster rollouts because teams are not dependent on the work of other teams, and targeted delivery allows for rapid, accurate feedback. In the GitHub case study we present in the next chapter, we can see how autonomy is key to their success by enabling developers to contribute meaningful changes quickly and allowing consumer-developers to collaborate on a single project asynchronously.

How Do We Get to Autonomy?

Making autonomy work requires good-enough knowledge for everyone doing the work. Seeking perfect information often delays decisions until they're no longer relevant or useful. At some point, we have to stop trying to measure and just get started. Don't let perfect be the enemy of good.

The less it costs to make a decision, the easier it is to empower someone to be autonomous. The cost exists on both sides of the decision point. Before we decide, we have to gather data and place it in context. The more that is pre-structured or predictable, the less cognitive work is required to do that contextualizing. The other cost is dealing with the results of the decision. If a decision is irreversible, widespread, or changes the experience significantly, it must have more consideration and review. This is especially true if it's not predictable how the changes will play out.

It is easy to decide which light switch to flip in your home. The options are accessible, you're already in the context of "using household electricity," and the consequences of illuminating one room versus another rarely have long-term significance. On the other hand, it is hard to choose which house to buy. It's a significant commitment, there are a lot of different data points, and you cannot really foresee what will happen in the lifespan of a mortgage.

Technology is similar—it's easier to choose a laptop model than a company's code stack. A laptop is easy to replace, but a code stack is not, and it requires a longer commitment.

Autonomy works best when people have the information they need for the scope of decision they're making. Today, our software often builds in these warnings: "If you click delete, this photo will be gone forever." Offering predictive estimates, small tests, and low-stakes bets allows everyone to practice making decisions, learn from context, and get better at judging results and outcomes. As they get more practice at autonomous decisions, they get better at judging the amount of information they have or need for new decisions.

The Path to Autonomy

The path to autonomy is not a tooling issue, or not only a tooling issue. It's, at least in part, a cultural issue. Many organizations are already on the path to autonomy, because autonomy is the foundational concept of Agile software development. Teams may be accustomed to deciding on their tasks for the next work period, or individuals may be free to implement solutions within the parameters of their requirements. It's a start.

The next step is making sure each autonomous unit knows the overall goal and requirements and supports them in choosing the amount of work they decide to take on. An experienced leader respects those estimates but also encourages teams to remember to account for the inevitable friction of humanity—sick days, train strikes, pandemics, and coffee emergencies. No plan survives first contact with reality, but thoughtful autonomy does allow people to accomplish what they committed to in almost all circumstances.

Context is part of making decisions, but we don't need to know everything if the system is set up to operate semi-independently. As with APIs, microservices, and promise theory (a framework for specifying the inputs and outputs of a system element instead of internal processes), you don't need to know how everything works, just how everything interacts. This independence of operation removes the toil and memory overhead of everything that is not directly relevant to the goal. It also makes it easier to swap things out, as long as the interfaces remain compatible.

Once work is done, or at least stopped, it needs to be managed some more: Does it meet the standards set? Should it be handed off to the next team? Is it fit for purpose? Does it match the current alignment? What is the next step? This natural progression of trying to measure outcomes and create focus on next steps provides an explanation as to why the next "A" is alignment.

Progressive Delivery is not just a constant ripple of changes out to users as different teams push their product out into the world. It is also the ripple back that tells teams how they did, what's next, what should be changed, fixed, or altered. It is as much a conversation and management opportunity as anything that happens internally.

The Benefits of Autonomy

As mentioned earlier, the drive for developer autonomy is primarily motivated by the desire for developer efficiency and developer happiness. According to the 2022 *State of the Developer Report* by Atlassian, "greater autonomy improves job satisfaction, speed of delivery, and team agility."[6]

Lack of autonomy is cited as one of the core causes of burnout, as described by Christina Maslach in her definitional work,[7] and the presence of autonomy is a component of feeling engaged and motivated as described by Daniel Pink in his book *Drive*. According to the 2018 *DORA Accelerate: State of DevOps Report*, "Autonomy has additional benefits. It leads teams to voice their opinions about their work, the team, and suggestions to improve the work. This transparent communication helps improve organizational culture as well."[8]

Empowering people with knowledge close to their decision points makes decisions faster and sounder, as described in David Marquet's leadership book based on his Navy service, *Turn the Ship Around*.[9] Leaders can also match the decisions and degree of importance. You shouldn't need a developer to change a single user's experience once it's programmed—that can be the support staff, or even the user. When you have hundreds, thousands, or millions of users, you don't want your developers doing password resets.

Radical Delegation

Practicing autonomy successfully, especially at scale, requires the use of radical delegation. The term "radical delegation" in relation to Progressive Delivery describes the release side of software delivery. With Progressive Delivery, our goal is a strict separation between the deployment of code to production and the release of features to users. In the spirit of enabling people to successfully engage in this practice, we need to provide a clear definition and a process, or framework, for implementation, assessment, and improvement. Thus, implementing radical delegation also benefits Progressive Delivery overall.

In the early iterations of Progressive Delivery, we just used the word "delegation." Later, we updated this to radical delegation, as the term better aligns with Admiral John Richardson's description of the United States Navy's practices.[10] Progressive Delivery requires true delegation, not abdication of responsibility. We adopted the term "radical" to emphasize that once authority is delegated, the decision-making power permanently resides with the delegated party, though accountability remains with leadership.

The key distinction is that responsibility remains with leadership even when they grant authority to others. Authority can be transferred; accountability cannot.

Admiral Richardson shares this example from the US Navy Regulations:

> *The responsibility of the Commanding Officer for his or her command is absolute, except when, and to the extent to which, he or she has been relieved therefrom by competent authority, or as provided otherwise in these regulations. The authority of the Commanding Officer is commensurate with his or her responsibility. While the Commanding Officer may, at his or her discretion, and when not contrary to law or regulations, delegate authority to subordinates for the execution of details, such delegation of authority shall in no way relieve the commanding officer of continued responsibility for the safety, well-being and efficiency of the entire command.*[11]

Radical delegation encapsulates both the task and the owner with the authority for the outcome. This does not transfer the responsibility for the outcome. The separation of authority and responsibility provides greater accountability and control. This separation is increasingly important as authority is shifted closer and closer to the end user.

In the naval context of ships at sea, radical delegation allowed a commander to delegate an objective to a captain, for example, to meet at these coordinates at this time. The authority on the ship belongs with the captain, but the responsibility for the ship's arrival still resides with the commander.

For those building software, radical delegation allows a customer success manager to turn on a new feature for a specific customer when the customer is ready for it. The authority to determine readiness belongs to the business owner (or person communicating with the user) who is closest to the user, but the responsibility for the feature working still resides with the engineers who build it and the operators who support the service.

In both cases, the delegation not only includes the "task" but also explicitly identifies the individual with authority. Both of these aspects are required for radical delegation.

In the early days of defining Progressive Delivery, we articulated two core tenets:

1. **Release progression:** progressively increasing the number of users who are able to see (and are impacted by) new features.
2. **Radical delegation:** progressively delegating the control of access to a feature to the owner who is closest to the outcome.

These two concepts continue to play a crucial role in autonomy. In order for the user to gain the benefits of autonomy (the right experience at the right time), the software builder needs to provide a control point that can be managed by the person closest to the user's needs.

Radical delegation is a framework for defining three aspects of autonomy: 1) The owner of control. 2) The feature/component to be controlled (or task to be accomplished). 3) The constraints or limits of the control.

Tossing things over the wall is an anti-pattern. The goal is to follow the DevOps principle of clear ownership and well-communicated handoffs. At the same time, having the responsibility remain with the developers who built the feature and the operations team that runs the infrastructure encourages shared investment in the user's outcome.

Radical delegation in software depends on trust and assurance. Trust is built, but assurance can be baked in with small releases, easy rollbacks, and predictions about who will be affected. This is why autonomy is difficult in low-trust environments. Radical delegation gives you the ability to better deliver the right product to the right people at the right time.

Psychological Safety

Psychological safety, a term first introduced as early as 1954 but popularized by Amy Edmondson for the modern work context,[12] is an organizational value that allows and even encourages team members to take risks and make mistakes without fear of personal repercussions. This is essential to autonomy, since without the ability to take risks or make mistakes safely, a team may not feel comfortable acting on the autonomy they have.

Even in large companies, individuals may have the ability to act autonomously due to a lack of actual security controls that limit actions. Many organizations rely on processes and fear to restrict changes that could have a negative impact on users. The process typically amounts to asking for permission. If you have to ask permission for everything, you are not acting on the system; you're a tool being used by your management. That kind of powerlessness makes toddlers lie screaming in the middle of the floor. Do we want to subject our peers to this type of excessive control and futility?

If a decision has large consequences, or unknowable consequences, it's rightfully more stressful to make it. None of us likes being wrong, and the more consequences it has, the more we avoid the risk of deciding the "wrong" way. This kind of paralysis leads both people and companies into a dangerous stasis, where the avoidance of risk becomes more important than any of the stated goals.

In the 1986 Challenger disaster, retrospective investigation found that individuals were aware of the risks presented by the O-rings in colder weather. Sadly, their input was ignored or minimized because it was important to the Morton-Thiokol organization that the company be seen as reliable and not give "false alarms." In a psychologically safe organization, those concerns could have been presented and addressed without the fear of employment termination.

The solution to this lack of safety is to make it safer to be autonomous, not to deprive people of the power to screw up. The power to screw up is the same as the power to make something better. We just need to make screwing up harder, or less catastrophic. Some ways to make possible mistakes less intimidating, easier to catch, and faster to correct include smaller releases and changes, a feature management platform that also provides excellent feedback, well-defined role-based access control (RBAC), peer review, clear audit logging, automated testing, and staged deployments.

Reversibility and Impact Prediction

We know mistakes will happen. Making mistakes less costly is a benefit, as well as a goal, of most software development frameworks. The cost of mistakes can be either quantitative or qualitative. A quantitative example could be a bank that makes a change to its trading algorithm and loses $460 million in thirty minutes. Qualitative costs could be a change made by a developer that caused a service outage, which leads to customer frustration. For autonomy to be done well, systems need to be built to minimize the cost of mistakes while encouraging the positive and generative information we may gain from "mistakes."

For cost, we need to consider two things:

1. Reversibility: What would it take to undo a change?
2. Impact prediction: What is the sphere of influence of the change?

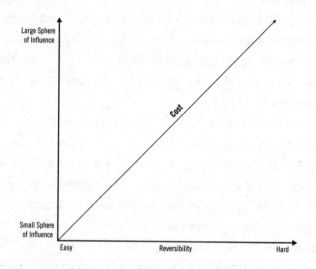

FIGURE 4.2: Prediction of Cost Based on Reversibility and Impact

As Figure 4.2 indicates, the harder changes are to reverse, and the greater the impact of the change, the more it will cost if things go sideways. Continuous delivery requires the practice of small changes, in part, for this reason. The cost of making a bad change when it is small is relatively low.

This is one benefit of canary deployments. Canary deployments roll out a change to a small percentage of systems or users (typically 1% or less) to limit the impact of things going poorly. Using a canary deployment to progressively deliver through a feature management platform greatly reduces the cost of any mistakes. This provides a central repository visible to everyone that clearly defines an owner who can make changes for the user and a clear understanding of the experience the user is having at any point in time. This level of visibility also provides the benefit of significantly reducing risks associated with making change.

In the next chapter's GitHub case study, we show how giving developers the ability to deploy autonomously to production can be extremely low risk. This gives developers a much more accurate view of how their changes will behave in the real world. GitHub developers then use feature management to expose features to a small number of users, gauge reaction, and detect problems in a safer way. Any change that is made through the feature management platform can be reverted quickly and easily through the use of feature flags. Because of the ability to progressively roll out or expose any changes to individual users or isolated audiences, the impact of a change can be tested in a production environment with zero risk to actual customers.

In the case study, we'll see just how fundamental this type of system was to GitHub's ability to deliver hundreds of changes a day while at the same time significantly reducing the cost of any mistakes. This ability to eliminate risk from the deployment and release process also significantly increases the psychological safety for the individuals and teams responsible for building and operating applications and services, regardless of scale.

Autonomy with safety builds trust between parties, and that trust leads to greater opportunities for autonomy. Risk is often associated with the cost of a mistake, as in Figure 4.2, but psychological safety builds autonomy, allowing us to make better decisions in planning and in the moment. We want to reduce opportunity cost and optimize for upside through lower-cost risk-taking.

Progressive Delivery allows us to answer the question: Should we ship new products and services on a Friday? The answer is, of course, yes, because we've done the work from a process and tools perspective to mitigate the risks of doing so. If you can't ship on a Friday, and you can't ship on the weekend, that only leaves four days a week to ship anything new. With Progressive Delivery, deployment freezes really shouldn't be a thing.

Challenges and Considerations on Autonomy

Autonomy Without Alignment

In Progressive Delivery, autonomy and alignment are always tightly coupled because they work best together. Alignment gives us the substance of what we are working together to do, and autonomy gives us the freedom to execute it. Without alignment, you have anarchy, or at least lots of movement without much progress.

Most of us have worked on that team at some point, or with that coworker. They have a vision, and they're going to work on it, whether or not that vision actually helps the goals of the team or the company. It's not quite the same as the popular conception of anarchy, because they are usually doing work that is at least adjacent to the work of the team, and they are seldom openly defiant; it's just that when you ask them for their work product, somehow, it's consistently not what you need for the next part of the process.

Downside of Autonomy

The downside of autonomy is management. It seems like the drawback might be chaos, but chaos is easier to solve than the reality that giving people the power to make choices means they must make choices. There is a lot of cognitive work in deciding what to do, how to do it, and how to tell if you did what you meant to do. Autonomous teams and people spend much more time communicating than in command-and-control structures. Communication takes time and effort, and sometimes it feels like you spend more time negotiating than creating. And sometimes this is true. That's the downside.

Everything we have learned about creative work, including software, tells us that conversations that feel like "wasted time" and "friction" are, in fact, "The Work." If we do them, we end up with better products faster, and happier teams. From Hicks's "Psychological Affordances," we see that:

The social context of the developer experience is much larger than interpersonal interaction. Like all people, developers working on software teams aim to meet foundational psychological needs, such as feeling safe, understood, and included, and achieving self-integrity. Access to these needs is shaped by social context and required to unlock high-quality, innovative collaborative knowledge work.[13]

Collaboration requires that everyone have some degree of autonomy and some differences of opinion because reconciling all the differences while you're working means you have already solved a bunch of problems that would appear when you deliver to a larger audience.

We don't really have a better name for the work of organizing, taking notes, clarifying group decisions, and making people talk to each other than "management." In the extremely life-critical case of airline pilots, it's called "crew resource management." Operating rooms have also adopted the same conventions. In software delivery, we often refer to this practice as defining constraints or establishing guardrails.

You are going to have to do management to get results from autonomy, even if it's nowhere in your title or official job duties.

Trust, Delegation, and Abdication

Autonomy requires trust. Trust in the competence and good intent of others, trust in the alignment of the team, and trust in yourself. This also mirrors other research, which shows that team dynamics are much more important to team effectiveness than a particular set of skills among team members. When researchers at Google studied over 180 engineering teams, they found that the most important factor in predicting a high-performing team was psychological safety or feeling safe taking risks around your team.[14] This was followed by dependability, structure and clarity of work, meaning, and impact. When teams have a good dynamic, their work benefits at the technological and organizational levels. Our own experience has confirmed this for several years, and we caution organizations not to ignore the importance of their people and their culture in technology transformations.

It can be difficult to shift your mindset from taking directions on how to accomplish a task to confidently making your own plan within your skill set to accomplish that task. It's one thing to be able to follow a code sample and swap in your own API endpoints or settings. It's a kind of independence, and you can get a lot done that way, but it's not the same as being able to construct novel code that does what you want. Code modification is a subset of autonomous coding. Without practice on the intervening steps between "fiddling with the sample" and "writing fully formed applications," it is not clear how to get from one to the other.

Trusting yourself to form a plan and execute it with skills you have or can acquire is hard, especially the first time. This does get easier as you learn what good looks like. But transferring this knowledge and confidence to others doing it the first time starts to look a lot like management—at least the positive intent of good management.

Trusting others to do the same thing may be even harder. But that's what we need to make autonomous teams work—we have to trust other people to create things that will match up with the things we create. The more we try to manage—or control—their process, the slower the process is, until it's so inefficient you might as well be doing everything yourself.

Delegation, on the other hand, is when you trust others to complete a task but retain the responsibility for the outcome (as we talked about earlier in the section on radical delegation). As the manager, you evaluate an objective, break it down into tasks, and divide the tasks among the members of your team to gain the benefit of parallel work. However, the overall outcome when the parallel workstreams are recombined is your responsibility.

Delegation requires bidirectional trust. The manager trusts the team to do the work that is needed to achieve the larger outcome. Meanwhile, the team members trust the manager to provide the proper level of context and clarity to enable individuals to successfully complete their tasks in a way that will successfully recombine.

Trust and delegation are not the same as abdication, though. Delegation requires alignment, either with a larger goal or with interoperability standards. This is because the manager who is delegating retains responsibility for the overall outcome. Abdication results when the manager relinquishes responsibility for the overall outcome.

Abdication is often an unintended result when you don't set standards for success or failure and don't provide a path to success. "Just fix it" is not helpful if the person you're talking to doesn't know what "fixed" is. In the context of an autonomous team, this frequently leads to duplication of effort, competitive behavior, fear of failure, and brittle systems.

Getting Started with Autonomy

Realizing and recognizing abundance is often the first step in Progressive Delivery. Autonomy typically comes soon after. Autonomy is people making the decisions they need to freely create, solve, and scale. Autonomy without alignment, however, carries a high risk that people can put in a lot of effort without achieving any tangible, useful work results for the organization.

Evaluating for Autonomy

Autonomy requires trust and delegation, but it is not abdication. Without some form of alignment where there are agreed-upon expectations and standards for success, autonomy can quickly become anarchy. We'll explore alignment in Chapter 6. For now, as you evaluate how autonomy can help your organization move faster, here are some questions to consider:

- Where are the bottlenecks that prevent you from delivering as you need?
- How much room do you have to deliver value within the confines of the larger organization?
- Can you change, fix, or alter something without permission?
- How do you share information or data critical to projects you are responsible for?
- Are you encouraged to communicate with your peers on other teams, as well as on your own team?

- What are the quality gates to allow a deployment? Who needs to approve a release? Who are the people and teams who can approve and promote new features?
- What amount of company money can you spend without getting pre-approval?
- Can you set meetings or request time from others without the permission of management? Can you decline meetings?
- Can you deploy to testing instances?
- Do you get to decide what you do in a day?
- Do you get to decide how to implement your work?
- How decoupled are you?
- Can you connect your work to user value?
- Can you say no to something without significant job repercussions?
- Can people pick their own tools/environment/location?
- Can people get creative?
- Do great ideas get ingested (such as from hackathons)?
- Can you set your working schedule and location?
- Are juniors getting the support they need?

Tools and Practices That Enable Autonomy

When thinking about how to extend or receive autonomy, there are tools and practices that many organizations have found helpful. Here's a short list to consider as you explore what might fit within your practices:

- Git
- feature flags that minimize the risk of trunk-based development
- feature flags that separate release from deployment
- Agile methodology
- DevOps methodology
- CI/CD methodology
- CI/CD platforms
- coding assistants

- blameless culture
- microservice architecture

Conclusion

Each of the four A's of Progressive Delivery reinforces and enables progress in the others. None of them can be fully "finished," and this is particularly true for autonomy. As we've seen throughout this chapter, software work has evolved from tightly controlled, sequential processes to distributed, parallel workflows that empower both developers and users.

Autonomy operates on multiple levels within an organization and its technology systems. For developers, it means the freedom to build, test, and deploy without unnecessary friction. For users, it means control over the pace of change and the ability to adopt new features at a comfortable rate. For a business, it could mean the visibility into what is happening with a product and its users. Throughout all these contexts, autonomy serves as a crucial counterbalance to technological jerk, allowing both makers and users of software to control the pace of acceleration rather than being thrown off balance by sudden changes.

The challenge is finding the right balance between autonomy and alignment. Too much unconstrained autonomy can lead to chaos and fragmentation; too little creates bottlenecks and resistance. Progressive Delivery offers a framework for achieving this balance through clear interfaces, feature management, and radical delegation that empowers the right people to make decisions at the right time.

Modern software delivery works because we have an abundance of software and network resources coupled with the autonomy to find the best path to solve a problem. This autonomy must exist within the context of alignment to work within a distributed system, and it requires automation to preserve our energy for novel and challenging tasks. Through Progressive Delivery, we can ensure that autonomy serves both the creators and consumers of technology, making change not just possible but purposeful.

In the next chapter, we'll explore a case study from GitHub—a company that has leveraged autonomy to deliver hundreds of changes per day while maintaining a positive experience for millions of developers worldwide. This practical example demonstrates how the principles of autonomy discussed in this chapter can be applied to create resilient, adaptive systems built to deliver the right thing to the right people at the right time.

Chapter 5

CASE STUDY: GITHUB

Now that we've explored the concept of autonomy in Progressive Delivery, let's take a look at a case study that highlights the concept in action. GitHub started as a friendly interface for a revolutionary but notoriously difficult source control program called Git. In time, GitHub came to incorporate many more features, such as conversations, visual diff tracking, web pages, and AI coding assistance. Distributed, asynchronous source control changed the relative power of managers and developers and coincided with a massive increase in developer autonomy. GitHub used this expansion of power to understand and deliver what their users wanted, instead of previous source control solutions, which had focused exclusively on what organizations wanted.

In its early years, GitHub was an unusual company organizationally. Its structure was very flat, and the employee community was extremely distributed. Remote work was the norm and the expectation. It was entirely natural that a company building tools that enable asynchronous and autonomous work across code bases would optimize for those very same things.

Situation

GitHub caught the wave of rising developer autonomy by allowing its developers to make application changes quickly and safely. This speed and flexibility made GitHub one of the fastest-growing cloud businesses of all time.

Complication

Autonomy within the GitHub organization and as part of the product required a balance between two simultaneous needs:

1. The rapid scale-up of GitHub's service to more users and larger companies. This meant GitHub needed to support a spectrum of users from fast first adopters to slower stable companies, all of whom considered the GitHub platform a part of their mission-critical infrastructure.
2. Developers and employees at GitHub who wanted to innovate and deliver valuable features and products as quickly as possible.

Users of the GitHub service both loved and feared the pace of innovation. Creators of technical innovations at GitHub championed innovation that was increasingly divergent from the core product. If changes were too disruptive, it might drive customers away or reduce the pace of adoption. If changes were too difficult to make, GitHub might miss their chance to lead the market.

Question

If an organization has abundant resources, how does it fuel innovation by enabling developers' autonomy? How do you appropriately incorporate alignment and automation to create a Progressive Delivery environment?

Answer

GitHub introduced feature flags and prioritized projects to automate the easy path ("move fast and fix things") for developers and operators working with ChatOps and end-to-end observability. These process changes resulted in the complete separation of code deployment and release and represent a quantitative experimental approach to product changes and feature adoption.

Abundance for All Developers

As we discussed in the previous chapter, Git was a key technology that enabled autonomy by reducing the cost of code branching, enabling parallel work.

When GitHub offered a cloud-based centralized service, they made autonomous, decentralized work possible and even normal. Teams working on projects no longer had to be in the same room, building, or even the same country.

Another key to GitHub's growth that relates to autonomy and Progressive Delivery was the decision to offer public repositories (online storage for code) free of charge. This was an enormous incentive for individuals and teams working on open-source software (OSS) across the globe to move their projects to GitHub. The autonomous nature of Git, coupled with the cloud-based GitHub service, was directly responsible for the exponential growth of OSS.

Developer experience and ergonomics were a constant priority. A great example of this was a chat we conducted with Sam Lambert, an early GitHub employee, in 2024. As he put it,

Everything was deployable from a command line in chat, and this was all the way back in 2008. GitHub was just obsessed with software being deployed very, very quickly and iteratively. And it started off without actually that much checking. You don't need to have all these things, like automated smoke tests, to be able to go and do this because you can break changes down that are really small and then do feature flagging, which is the best way to do stuff right now.[1]

In the early days, everyone in the company used GitHub for collaboration. Most employees were developers themselves and were building the product that they wanted to use. Autonomy was key to making this collaboration an asset instead of a liability for developer experience and workflows. Every person with an idea could work on it independently, in the open, and then solicit and incorporate feedback from others without interrupting their flow.

In general, developers (like most people who create things) are highly motivated when they can work at their own pace and ship new code, features, and products. Git branching optimized this ability to work autonomously and quickly. As we mentioned in the last chapter, prior to Git, developers often needed to wait for each other to move work forward. Or, if they worked in parallel (two or more developers working on the same section of code), there would inevitably be a required pause in work to merge (or combine all the changes from various developers) all the branches of a code tree back into the trunk (or main). Prior to Git merging, it was not uncommon for code freezes (pauses in development when merging was done) to last for months, especially for large code bases.

GitHub took these improvements a step further with GitHub Flow. GitHub Flow is a work process optimized for maximum time spent actually writing code and minimal context switching and waiting. This was the recommended development framework when working with GitHub and aligns with how the product was built.[2]

In addition to GitHub's optimized approach to developer autonomy, they also innovated in other key areas to become one of the first organizations to practice Progressive Delivery of software at scale in the form of a feature flagging service, Flipper, that could be incorporated into every code change. Feature flags were the key enabling technology, in combination with Git, that allowed GitHub to move at the pace it did.

As Lambert described,

We had something called Flipper, which was very early in the Ruby community. It just looks at what you're allowed to see, very simply, in the database and gives you access to it. I think feature flags are essential for Progressive Delivery, for this way of continually deploying. Because it needs to be the actual gate for what people see. And then you need to be able to fill up behind the gate continually by shipping software.

For GitHub, shipping was everything. The entire culture of the company is identified with shipping software. "We would deploy GitHub[.com] sometimes over a hundred times in a day, and this was in 2008," said Lambert. "GitHub started in 2008, and it started with a very iterative kind of approach to software development, obviously using pull requests to go and do that. And that became an immovable part of the culture. You could not change this."

Aligning All the Stars

As the number of internal developers grew and the GitHub.com service expanded, the culture of shipping persisted. Feature flags and Git were critical components for making use of the abundance of resources and expanding the autonomy of developers. Feature flags also did a lot of the heavy lifting to align the sheer volume of code changes with the desire to provide a delightful developer experience. While feature flags allowed developers to deploy their code changes over a hundred times a day, but they still had to align on who could see those changes and when was the right time to deploy for the right audience.

ChatOps was the differentiator, according to Lambert: "Progressive Delivery at GitHub and ChatOps were joined at the hip. Like, everything was done in chat. This has never left GitHub though. And I always think about this. People have tried to make ChatOps a thing a number of times at a number of companies, and it has never worked [as well]."

According to Lambert, ChatOps wasn't just a tool at GitHub, it was part of the culture:

I think it was partly because GitHub's culture mandated everything going into chat or written form. Nothing was done in person. When I joined, even if you were in the office, you would [have discussions in chat] to not exclude people

working remotely. But what that meant was you had this environment where,
for example, debugging was done live, and if you could pull up graphs, charts,
anything you wanted to see, could just get pulled into chat. GitHub's hardest
working employee [wasn't] a person, it was the chatbot called Hubot.

Chat was an amazing way to create both visibility and alignment, and
Hubot was also the automation engine for everything. This is how GitHub
was able to practice Progressive Delivery.

AI, Agents, and Autonomy

We also talked to GitHub CEO Thomas Dohmke. He said the rise of LLMs
meant Progressive Delivery techniques were essential—using observability
to understand how models behave in terms of user experience, with respect
to model choice and managing transitions to new models from LLM providers such as Anthropic, when their older versions are deprecated.

I think the way to think about Progressive Delivery is that it's no longer optional.
You have to do it, because otherwise you can never upgrade to the next model,
because you're never going to collect enough data in your internal testing to
decide whether that new model is actually better than the previous model.

Measurement and data is critical in "what if" scenarios. Coding and
release is now experimentation. As such, Dohmke said we're going to need
autonomous AI agents—a continuous delivery agent, an agent watching
A/B tests, a feature flagging agent—to help make these decisions and help
you make sense of the vast number of data points you're collecting. Progressive Delivery agents are coming, and that is going to bring an entirely
new frontier in autonomy.

Progressively Shipping, Continually Deploying

Deploying code is not the same as releasing code. In Lambert's words, "You
separate deploying code to shipping a feature. Those two things are very

separate." An additional distinction at GitHub was that "shipping a feature" did not mean the new code was visible to everyone all at once. The feature flag service, Flipper, allowed the team to have more granular control of who could see various parts of the shipped code.

By separating the deployment of code into production from shipping features to users, GitHub had the ability to maintain operational excellence in its production environment and choose which version of its product was available to which of its users at any given point in time.

This basic separation allowed the developer to autonomously deploy to production whenever they wanted without any risk. They also had the ability to control who saw what and when. In the case of GitHub, the next step was to start to understand which users were actually ready for the new features and how they were adopting them.

Summary

Autonomy represents a critical evolution in software development, transforming how teams create and deliver technology. By empowering developers to make independent decisions within a framework of shared goals and constraints, organizations can unlock unprecedented levels of innovation, efficiency, and employee satisfaction. The key lies not in unchecked freedom but in creating an environment of trust, clear communication, and well-defined boundaries that enable individuals to act decisively and creatively.

The journey toward true autonomy requires a fundamental cultural shift, moving beyond traditional command-and-control structures to embrace radical delegation and psychological safety. Tools like feature flags, microservices, and robust communication platforms facilitate this transformation, allowing teams to deploy code rapidly while maintaining the flexibility to manage user experiences with precision. As demonstrated by the GitHub case study, successful autonomy is not about eliminating oversight, but about creating intelligent systems that support individual initiative while maintaining alignment with broader organizational objectives.

Just Because You Can, Doesn't Mean You Should

Without alignment, autonomy can fall into anarchy. Alignment between developers can help ensure products and services run well and that duplication of effort is minimal. This is a great way to promote operational excellence in your development organization. With Progressive Delivery, we also want to consider alignment in a much broader context—alignment with the needs of the user of your product or service.

In the next chapter, we'll go deeper into this topic and explore how Progressive Delivery can help you get better at building the right things to start with, instead of just hoping you find the right users at the right time. After all, if your users don't want the feature you're building, there is likely never a "right" time to deliver it.

Chapter 6
ALIGNMENT

If you want to build a ship, don't drum up people to collect wood and don't
assign them tasks and work, but rather teach them to long for the endless
immensity of the sea.

—**Antoine de Saint-Exupéry**

If jerk in physics is the sudden, unexpected change in acceleration that
throws us off balance, and abundance is our technological potential energy,
autonomy our force vectors, then alignment is the frame of reference—a
set of coordinates that when shared determines the position, velocity, and
direction of all objects in that frame. As software makers, we've spent more
than thirty years optimizing how we build software. Now we need to get
better at how we deliver it.

Just as physicists use the concept of force vectors to describe the magnitude and direction of a force, alignment in software development provides a frame of reference, forcing everyone to see from the same perspective. Your frame of reference keeps everything inside moving in the same
direction, at least relative to the things outside your frame.

Without alignment, the potential energy of abundance and the loosely
coupled force vectors of autonomy would result in increasing entropy—
chaotic motion—like bumper cars with drivers each steering in different
directions, creating a series of jarring, unpredictable jerks that leave pas-
sengers disoriented and unable to reach their destination.

When alignment is weak, all the abundance and autonomy in the
world will simply amplify technological jerks. Teams move quickly but in
conflicting directions, creating a system where change happens constantly
but progress remains elusive. The resulting motion sickness affects not
just development teams but ripples outward to users who experience these

technological jerks as inconsistent interfaces, unpredictable features, end-less updates, and frustrating workflow disruptions.

Effective alignment transforms these competing forces into coordi-nated motion. In Progressive Delivery, alignment is the frame of reference that brings everyone together into a shared perspective. Like when you're all riding in the same car. Inside the car you can easily pass snacks back and forth and have conversation. While outside the car it's really challenging to coordinate simple handoffs and communication. Having the same frame of reference allows us to leverage our technological potential energy for our products to deliver the greatest value to our users. Without it, we might do work, but we are unlikely to make progress.

> **a·lign·ment (/ə'līnmənt/):** Focusing resources responsible for developing software to all work in the same direction.

In the context of Progressive Delivery, alignment is one of the two ways to wrangle abundance and autonomy by reducing or limiting the variability of what is created. In Progressive Delivery, both alignment and automation are centered around the user experience. For alignment, this means we are looking to center on the users' needs.

Alignment isn't the same as agreement or cooperation, although it can include those elements. It's not unity or unanimity, either. Instead, it is the active, collective choice to make your vectors (direction and movement) match. The moment of being aligned is a snapshot of a dynamic state.

Unlike business alignment (which too often simply refers to agreeing with the people in management), alignment in software is about consider-ing the state and direction of our teams, our dependencies, and most of all, our users. The business needs to focus on the goal and communicate the goal and its value clearly to the builders. Where are we now, where are we going, and how can we do that together?

We can measure alignment quantitatively and qualitatively. Qualita-tive measurements can be achieved through surveys and interviews, while quantitative information can be sourced through monitoring usage rates and patterns in feature adoption and workflow completion. It is inter-esting to note that the qualitative measurements for alignment are the surveys and interviews with users. This is because the alignment pillar is focused on user experience. As Charity Majors, a pioneer of observability and Honeycomb founder, likes to say, "Nines don't matter if your users aren't happy."[1]

Alignment is also the pillar that moves us beyond our foundation in continuous integration and delivery (CI/CD) and into Progressive Delivery. Considering all our stakeholders as part of our alignment broadens the way we understand what we are making. We aren't building a solution; we're building a tool that will help a person solve a problem.

Including the human on the other side of our screens (the user) helps us make better tools. Instrumenting and integrating what we learn from users helps us avoid falling victim to the tendency to build something that is really designed to work only for ourselves. Alignment widens our understanding and gives us a way to partner with users instead of plundering them.

In this chapter, we will examine what alignment means in the context of Progressive Delivery and for whom. Software has always been about aligning the computer, the code, and the user. Sometimes that means thousands of developers across dozens of divisions to make an operating system, and sometimes it means one hobbyist building something for themselves. But in order to build the right thing for the right person, you have to understand what is needed and who you're building for.

Historical Context and Evolution of Alignment

Much of early software came from command-and-control environments. Admiral Grace Hopper was not a title distributed by a bridge club but by the US Navy. In the military crèche where software was born, it made sense that the purpose and outputs of software should be clearly defined before anything was created. As software expanded in capabilities, from decryption and trajectory calculation to communication, multidirectional inputs showed up. Software had to not only execute but also respond.

Commercial software experienced the same evolution, from a time when companies were in control of what software was used for to a time when software was useful to communicate back to the company. No longer was software something that was simply distributed. It became something that was uploaded.

When we first started separating software from hardware, it was a giant leap in understanding the alignment of our teams. Now we weren't all touching the same giant computer, and we needed to think about how a program would work for someone else. Naturally, we designed software the same way we designed all technology at that point—by specifying what it should do and not do, and planning it all out ahead of time. Gantt charts plotted out dependencies and specifications predicted dates and functionality. Software was distributed on physical media (like floppy disks and CDs), and each release was a large inflection point in how it worked.

Agile and test-driven delivery were born from that time in response to the feeling that "years" was a long time to wait to get business value to users. Instead, what if we broke software into smaller parts, called them stories, tied them to user actions, and spent less time planning things that inevitably got changed? The alignment changed from a "top-down building plan" to a more responsive, team-based system.

This paralleled the availability of much easier communication between parts of software. We might not have called them microservices at the beginning, but the idea of being able to pass data and requests from one part of the software to another through a standardized format accelerated the capabilities of teams to work independently and still be aligned.

DevOps emerged when the organizations making software realized they couldn't just ship physical media anymore. With the rise of software-as-a-service and web computing, it became their responsibility to make sure the software stayed running. That meant that "IT" wasn't just about internal support; they needed to be supporting the product for external use. And that responsibility went much better when operations and software were talking to and communicating with each other about the whole life cycle of the software, instead of thinking of "writing" and "delivery" as two distinct categories.

Aligning these two teams, and sometimes even making them the same team, did wonders to speed up the feedback loop around how the software actually behaved in the wild. One of the things organizations learned about releasing software from DevOps was that more frequent, smaller releases carried much less risk of catastrophic failure. This is evident from the research presented in the *State of DevOps Reports*.[2] It changed the idea of release.

Working back from that, it became clear that individual developers needed the autonomy to commit their changes and see them run through testing, integration, and deployment to understand the effect of what they had done. This required developers to build a set of skills that had previously not been their responsibility. To streamline this process, CI/CD became an organizational goal. A person should be able to run the software whenever they wish and know that they have a stable and releasable version. This requires a lot of automation, but also alignment—to be sure no one's work is off in a long-running branch, unmerged and presenting risk.

CI/CD operationalized the movement of a feature from the developer through testing and deployment, so it was possible for the developer to see their changes in production or near-production conditions almost instantly. Shortening the time from work to results greatly increased the effectiveness of developers by allowing them to retain context and understanding.

Progressive Delivery extends CI/CD's immediate feedback benefits by adding user observability to the array of information available to the developer and the organization.

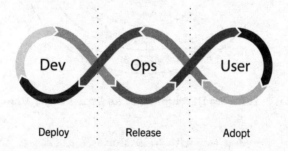

FIGURE 6.1: The Progressive Delivery Cycle

The DevOps infinity loop is familiar to many practitioners. Progressive Delivery extends this to include users, who supply important information back to both the operations and development loops. This extension can be visualized, as in Figure 6.1, which we have named the Progressive Delivery cycle. Operations is frequently charged with collecting and displaying user metrics and telemetry. This information needs to make it to both operations (to improve the user experience of the product) and development (to improve both the product stability and performance for operations as well as the features and workflows for users).

Progressive Delivery is the understanding that all these advances are built around development and delivery. We have spent decades optimizing this part of the software development life cycle. (See Figure 6.2.) But there is another half we haven't included in our considerations—the user. The person who uses our software is an *essential* part of our alignment.

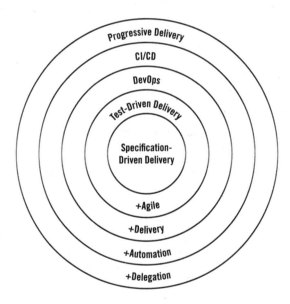

FIGURE 6.2: Software Development Life Cycle (SDLC) Onion Model

We have hinted at this with "user stories," "use cases," and "delivery metrics," but those are all outbound projections. It's time for us to align with users by allowing them to affect the way their software works, presents itself, and integrates into their lives. It's time to take all the metrics we have about use and apply them mindfully to what we're actually making. If you want to build the right thing for the right people at the right time, you have to break free of the push model of software delivery and embrace the conversation of human value.

Complexity and the Physics of Distributed Systems

As software development evolved from monolithic architectures to distributed systems, we faced a new challenge in alignment. By splitting our programming into server and client, data and operations, front- and back-end layers, we multiplied the complexity of getting everything to work together. The technological mass of our systems increased dramatically, creating new forms of inertia that required more sophisticated alignment mechanisms.

This fragmentation of software architecture paralleled a key physics principle: As systems gain more independent components, they require stronger organizing principles to prevent chaotic motion. The software industry's solution emerged in standardized interfaces and protocols that could coordinate these increasingly complex systems without requiring rigid centralization.

When Amazon promoted the idea of the 2-pizza team, they also talked about how every team would communicate with other parts of the organization with APIs. This represented a fundamental shift in alignment thinking—rather than forcing teams to follow identical processes or structures, they specified how the information would flow between them. The entire organization was aligned on using APIs to communicate anything that needed to pass between team or service boundaries.

We can see increased complexity like this through real-world examples in chemistry. The rules for chemistry are defined by the laws of physics, specifically how particles (primarily electrons, protons, and neutrons) attract or repel each other. Take, for example water. The molecule is held together by covalent bonds between elements, or the sharing of electrons. It turns out that covalent bonds, with their shared electrons, allow for a smooth transfer of energy between otherwise independent elements, making for more stable, less reactive molecules. So, forming connections via shared energy can make larger systems more stable. (See Figure 6.3 on page 88.)

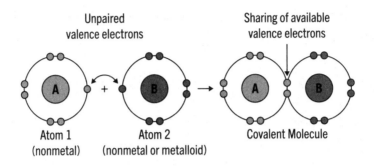

FIGURE 6.3: Covalent Bonds

If software has eaten the world, it has eaten humanity too—and we have become symbiotic with software. When we say socio-technical system, it isn't just the global software/humanity gestalt, but the systems within the greater system. The smaller the system, the easier it is to align. It's easier to schedule a meeting with one or two colleagues, and it becomes increasingly more difficult as you add more. Every time you extend the meeting to larger cohorts—your immediate team, your department, your business unit, and so on—you increase the difficulty of decision-making and alignment.

Software makers know that adding nodes adds complexity, but it's an inescapable complexity. It means alignment has to be stronger and less prescriptive. This is also a function of the level at which you experience the system.

For example, from the user's perspective, a search engine like Google or Bing is simple. You just type what you want to know. But from a system perspective, there is n-dimensional complexity to find results to be crawled and indexed, evaluated, and sorted for best result presentation. What ads should be served next to the results? And what feedback should be monitored and reported based on user behavior on the results page?

Building the trust that enables this strong alignment and weak direction is not easy from a command-and-control mindset. DevOps marked a cultural evolution that paralleled the technological one, both recognizing that in complex systems, alignment works best when it establishes boundaries and interfaces rather than dictating every detail of motion.

The Cookie (R)evolution

As software development evolved beyond physical media and into networked applications, a parallel revolution occurred in how we tracked and understood user behavior. Around the turn of the millennium, as the web matured from static pages into complex applications, a silent transformation in alignment began—one based not on organizational structures but on user data.

Marketing contains fearful wonders you may not know about. For more than twenty years, it has been easy for anyone who cares to look to see your browser type, your computer, your language, and dozens of other statistics about you. That capacity was built to help troubleshoot the weird problems that come with trying to create a universal experience for a hugely diverse viewing platform. Web 2.0 added even more information: what site you visited last, whether you were logged in and paying, where your mouse cursor went, or how much of a page you actually scrolled through. Dozens of data points, sometimes hundreds, for each page. Cookies allowed site owners and advertisers to deliver targeted ads across every site you went to since the ad space could be allocated as the page loaded.

This data revolution represented a fundamental shift in alignment possibilities. For the first time, software creators could directly observe user behavior at scale without explicit surveys or feedback sessions. The gap between what users said they wanted and what they actually did became measurable. Without knowing user intent, this behavioral data can be badly misinterpreted, but it is still an important movement forward in understanding. This implicit feedback loop transformed how software teams aligned with user needs, creating a continuous data stream that could inform development priorities.

While some very dedicated people try to lock down the telemetry their browsers, phones, and computers emit, it's a losing battle unless you spend a lot of time on it. It's no exaggeration to say there are enough data points on all of us to build out extremely complete social graphs, interest patterns, and predictive behavior models.

For software creators, this alignment in observation rather than specification represents a critical evolutionary step toward the practice of Progressive Delivery, if we take advantage of it. For instance, we can allow the user to opt out as much as possible, and we can use the data for good. Data use and customer information can become a conversation, not just an extraction. Where earlier software development methodologies relied on predicting user needs up front, the cookie revolution enabled a responsive, data-driven approach that could continuously realign as user behavior evolved. This shift paralleled the move from monolithic releases to continuous delivery—both representing the software industry's growing recognition that alignment is not a static goal but a dynamic, ongoing process.

Hacking and Growth Mindset

Just as cookies transformed how we gathered data about users, users were also changing how they interacted with software during this time. Once it became possible for ordinary users to change software, they did. The relationship was becoming increasingly bidirectional—not only were software creators observing users, but users were beginning to modify and reshape software to better meet their needs. Early hacking was almost always an attempt to get software to align better with what the user wanted.

This user-driven modification represented a crucial shift in the alignment dynamic. Cookies allowed companies to silently observe behavior, and hacking and customization created direct, visible expressions of user needs. The distinction highlighted a fundamental tension in software alignment—passive data collection versus active user participation as part of shaping the experience.

Knowing what your software is doing is a surprisingly difficult problem in computer science. Almost all our stacks in the world are complex, and few of us understand every layer of them. One snippy letter from Ada Lovelace to Charles Babbage begs him not to alter things in a way that seems to improve them because it throws off her calculations.[3] The first debugging argument!

These early tensions between creators and users foreshadowed modern Progressive Delivery approaches, where alignment requires sophisticated telemetry and direct user control over feature adoption. As users gained technical sophistication and customization tools improved, the balance of power in the alignment relationship began to shift toward a more collaborative model.

This evolution of alignment—from rigid military specifications to user-driven adaptability—reflects our growing understanding that software isn't merely a tool we create and distribute, but a living system that must align with both its creators and users to truly succeed. Progressive Delivery represents the next step in this journey, embracing the reality that alignment must extend beyond the development team to include the full spectrum of constituents who interact with our software.

Key Principles and Applications

Why Alignment Matters

A modern operating system is far too massive for a single person or team to build. It requires specialist knowledge in dozens of fields, from drivers to security to machine language. Yet, we interact with operating systems on our computers, phones, and even in our cars without ever having to consider how they were made. Immense accomplishments don't require that every person knows and understands every part; they require that every person knows what the local and larger goal is and how they can contribute to it.

Alignment is one of the reasons remote work has been a difficult transition. It was—or at least seemed—easier to maintain alignment when people walked into the same building every day and apparently absorbed alignment with others via some type of osmosis. While that was certainly alignment on easy mode, it was seldom mindful alignment. It was an accident of time and space. Working remotely, we have to think about how alignment happens, and we have the opportunity to do it meaningfully.

The value of alignment is that it strengthens an organization. One piece of dry spaghetti is easy to break. A package of dry spaghetti is harder to break. Once you get to two packages, it's unreasonably difficult. The peril of very close alignment is that there's less resilience in other directions. Go ahead and try to snap aligned, dry macaroni noodles.

Brittle alignment leads to problems because any deviation is not seen as diversifying and strengthening, but as defying. Progressive Delivery is not advocating brittle alignment. Instead, we want alignment that functions more like a well-tuned orchestra, where musicians respond to both the conductor and to each other, adjusting their tempo and volume in real time. Each section contributes its unique voice to create a harmonious whole, but they also listen and adapt. In this model, the conductor doesn't dictate every note; they coordinate and respond to the ensemble's collective expression. When you find good alignment with your users, creators, market, and environment, it should feel like a dynamic conversation—each participant both leading and following, creating something greater than what any single party could produce alone.

Constituents in the product development and delivery conversation include engineering, product design, customer success, and your go-to-market team. Consider marketing's role within product delivery and adoption. With delegation, marketing can oversee when a product is released—this is autonomy. Successful marketing is concerned with how a product lands and thereby has a vested interest in observability—this is alignment. When constituents like marketing can collaborate with others to ensure combined success, this is Progressive Delivery.

Alignment Goals

It's hard to achieve alignment if you don't understand the goal. It's tempting to make alignment itself the goal, but that's how you get echo chambers and groupthink. The goal you're aligning to needs to be broad enough that everyone can see their place in it and narrow enough that they can tell what isn't part of the goal. When you get a goal that is well-defined, you can hold up every action and choice to it and tell whether it will help or hinder the goal.

Alignment to an overall goal helps groups within a company by keeping them from veering off into their own weird things. Alignment with customer needs and desires keeps a company from ignoring its own long-term interests. Especially in software, it's easy for us to get hypnotized by the potential of new, shiny things and forget that our assignment is to help users get things done. Alignment and frequent course corrections help us keep in touch with the people who want to be our users.

Good alignment is knowing what your company's business value is and how your daily and weekly work connects with that goal and with the people who use your product. For example, people working with Adobe products know that people pay for it to actualize their digital creativity. Incorporating AI into Photoshop to help retouch an image faster will increase the value of the software to the people who use it. Excellent alignment is also sitting with users on a regular basis to watch them use the software and see their realistic conditions, so you design for real users, not idealized ones.

Weak alignment is when you are not sure why you're making something or why it matters. When priorities change mid-cycle and you're asked to add an AI feature but not told why it's good for the company or the users, that's weak alignment. Even if AI might be useful in that situation, the lack of context and communication means you may add something that doesn't improve the product or user experience. Very bad alignment is when this happens across the whole organization, so you're adding two buttons that do almost identical things.

Who Are Your Constituents?

For us to achieve true alignment, we must first answer a fundamental question: With whom are we trying to align? Progressive Delivery is defined as getting the right thing to the right people at the right time in a way that is sustainable for everyone, but this definition depends critically on how we define "everyone." The traditional business approach is to refer to "stakeholders," the roles that appear in a thousand presentation slides. These avatars of developer, customer, management, and so on function pretty well to talk about broad groups, but they create an alignment boundary that's too narrow for effective Progressive Delivery.

Instead, we talk about constituents—a more inclusive concept that recognizes all participants in the ecosystem surrounding your product. Constituents aren't just passive recipients of your product; they're active participants whose needs, behaviors, and contexts shape what your product is and how it functions. There is no product without someone to use it, just as there is no product without someone to build it.

Think about medical records software—the stakeholders are developers, clinics, administrators, hospitals, and IT. But true alignment requires extending beyond these obvious groups to include the whole constellation of constituents: medical professionals who read records other doctors write, patients who use the portal to review test results, family members assisting with a loved one's care, and regulatory bodies overseeing data privacy.

These constituents don't appear on the conventional list of stakeholders, but their needs fundamentally influence how the software should function. Missing these alignment points creates software that technically works but fails to serve its broader ecosystem. Progressive Delivery requires alignment with this complete constituency, not just the officially recognized stakeholders who hold financial or organizational power.

By expanding your alignment horizon to encompass all constituents, you create a more robust alignment vector that directs your development efforts toward delivering value across the entire ecosystem, not just to the most visible or vocal participants. Keep your organizational goals in mind and limit feedback and modifications to what your team can afford to act on. Smaller changes will be easier to get feedback on, and thus easier for everyone to implement.

Benefits: Alignment in Action

Extending Control with Feature Flags

Feature flags and a feature management platform allow an organization to deliver features progressively. This is especially important when your users or end user constituents have vastly different needs or abilities regarding adoption patterns.

Feature flags efficiently provide different user cohorts with different experiences. When using feature flags to extend access to different features or visibility of different workflows, flags would be designed from the beginning to be long-running. These flags stay in the code as control points to modify the user experience long-term.

The advantage of having a feature management platform for this long-term use case is the flexibility to extend control of these experiences to different constituents within your ecosystem. Your support organization, customer success, or even marketing team can be given permission to control flags where appropriate. Using feature flags in this way provides clarity and visibility to the experiences your users are having. When we have a way to administer them so that we can accurately diagnose what feature flags users have on or off, we have a lot of insight into both the behavior of the software for that constituent and the software behavior that users prefer.

Global Observability

The only way to tell if a complex system is aligned is to observe it. We can't trust the diagrams to represent the truth—after all, the map is not the territory. Is it accepting the inputs we expect? Is it providing the outputs we expect? Is it consuming the resources we expect? Can we ask it questions? The difference between monitoring (watching for what you expect) and observability is that with observability, you can ask questions that you didn't expect to have.

Your database can send you a text when it starts overfilling. That's monitoring and alerting. You can see what has been written into it. That's logging. Being able to ask the question about why it keeps happening? That's observability.

We often think about observing computer systems and the behavior of our software in the world. However, for good alignment, we also need to observe socio-technical systems—the ones inside our organization and the ones created by our users. Without that rich input, we're not getting a real picture of our work and how it fits into the world.

Strategy

Alignment in architecture makes it easier for groups to communicate with each other and reach alignment in purpose. Once you set that as the goal, you can see how declaring that every subsystem must communicate by a documented API can serve to align local, system-wide, and global goals.

So, if the goal is strategic alignment, what are the steps that make it happen? First, you have to ask what your goal is, and crucially, whether it has been accurately communicated to all the people who can make it happen. Then, you have to make sure those people have both the resources (abundance) and the autonomy to make it happen, considering what they already need to do and how they feel about that. Next, you have to make sure that what you are producing works with itself and other parts of your product. Finally, you need to be sure that what you have made is accomplishing what you intended it to.

Defining Success

How do you know if alignment has worked? Well, what was the goal that you were aligning to, and have you accomplished it? Have you made measurable progress toward it? Is the work that your teams are doing contributing to it?

When you set a goal, you also set the success metrics that let you know whether you've accomplished it. Success metrics include things like "a user can accomplish their task" and "our business is not harmed," but also "20% user growth" and "team cooperation improved as measured by sentiment surveys."

What Users Need, When They Need It, at the Least Cost and Risk to Everyone

At its core, Progressive Delivery exists to serve a fundamental purpose that can be distilled into a simple yet powerful statement: delivering what users need when they need it for the right value and least risk to everyone involved.

This is perhaps the manifesto of Progressive Delivery—not a description of its methods but a declaration of its ultimate goal. It captures the essence of what we're trying to achieve when we implement these practices. By keeping this goal at the forefront of our thinking, we create a clear criterion against which all of our technical decisions, organizational structures, and delivery practices can be measured.

When we center our work on this purpose, we naturally align our teams, our technologies, and our processes toward creating value rather than just producing output. It transforms software delivery from the mechanical process of shipping features to a thoughtful practice of providing solutions that genuinely help people accomplish their goals.

We Need to Know Exactly What People Need

Delivering value requires understanding what users truly need, which can often differ from what they explicitly ask for. Users typically request features, but they're actually seeking outcomes or solutions. For example, a user might ask for "a faster search function," when their actual need is "finding critical information during customer calls without losing the customer's attention."

This deeper understanding requires us to look beyond workflows to workflow goals and beyond features to user outcomes. We must understand not just what users do with our software but why they do it and what success looks like for them. When building enterprise software, we need to understand not just our direct users but also their customers and stakeholders.

Capturing this understanding can't be a one-time exercise. We need mechanisms to encode user needs into our development process, whether through user stories, personas, or ongoing feedback loops and user observability. The most effective product teams maintain continuous conversations with users, updating their understanding as needs evolve and ensuring this knowledge shapes every subsequent decision.

When Will They Need It?

People don't always need everything right away. Progressive Delivery offers us the opportunity to tune the software we present to what is appropriate for the stage a user is at. One approach is to first build the most basic work-flow to accomplish a task. Then, over time, provide optionality to meet the needs of corner cases or an expanding number of users.

This resembles how modern electrical grids manage power: Rather than delivering the full voltage of transmission lines directly to homes (which would be catastrophic), transformers step down the power progressively to levels appropriate for different uses. Some buildings need industrial-level power, while residential areas need a fraction of that voltage, and sensitive electronics require even further regulation. The electrical system delivers precisely what's needed, where it's needed, when it's needed—neither overwhelming nor underpowering any component.

Part of delivering accurately is understanding specific needs and serving those. It is not what you think or expect people to need, but their actual needs that will be served by your product and features. Allowing people to choose their own path is one way to try to tailor this, but it's even more powerful when it's paired with an opinionated path that helps people see where they could or should go.

What Will It "Cost"?

Cost is obviously not just about the straightforward monetary expense of software. Everything has intangible costs, like behavior change, interaction friction, workflow alterations, and changing cognitive requirements. In the context of Progressive Delivery, understanding these costs helps us build the right thing for the right people at the right time in a sustainable way.

Yet, technology often reshapes our expectations rather than simply reducing our effort. Consider cloud storage: It was meant to free us from the constraints of physical storage limitations, and it did. But rather than simply storing the same amount of data more efficiently, we began keeping more...everything—drafts, versions, logs, backups of backups—because the abundance made it possible. The technological inertia of having unlimited storage changed our behavior patterns entirely.

We see this pattern throughout computing history. Email eliminated the manual labor of writing letters, but instead of sending the same number of messages more efficiently, we now process hundreds of communications daily. Video calls removed the need for physical travel, but instead of having the same number of meetings with less hassle, our calendars filled with more interactions than were ever possible before.

This isn't a criticism—it's a recognition that when we alter the physics of a system by introducing abundance or automation, we don't just make the existing work easier; we fundamentally change what work looks like and how much of it we expect to do. The technological jerk comes not just from the new capability but also from the shifting expectations that follow.

Integration testing shows a similar cost scenario. Testing all the pieces of software together on multiple platforms was once a very manual and time-intensive process that could add months to the software release timeline. It was a pain point ripe for automation, and companies arose to solve that problem. Now, even the smallest startups consider automated integration testing a normal part of their build pipeline.

The human labor of performing quality assurance (QA) has been almost entirely replaced, at least for that part of the process. But because automation became so easy, we changed the standards for what is acceptable. Now, instead of doing customized QA, someone has to own the build pipeline, keep it running, and furthermore keep the runtime down to the fastest time possible. There was a time when it wasn't notable that software took hours to build, but now we realize that the less time it takes to build, the more likely people are to build often and fix smaller problems faster.

There are also financial costs, both in up-front and opportunity costs. There are environmental costs to running inefficiently. There are language and translation costs, depending on how much of the world we want to include or exclude. Progressive Delivery allows us to manage these costs by incrementally introducing change, measuring impact, and adjusting our approach based on real user feedback.

We often talk about cost and risk as the same thing, as if money were the only way to calculate the value of something. However, it's important to identify risks as things that might not happen, but if they did, they would have a negative impact beyond mere finance. Life insurance may be able to make survivors' lives less tenuous, but it will never make up for grief and absence.

As software purveyors, we must acknowledge that there are some risks we take on that we can mitigate, and some that may be too dangerous to do at all. If we lose control of a serverless function, it may go rogue and run up a bill with a lot of zeros behind it. If we lose control of hate crime moderation, real people can die. That's not something that can or should be quantified by money. And yet, it takes money to mitigate that risk as much as possible. Progressive Delivery's approach of controlled, reversible rollouts is particularly valuable when managing these high-stakes risks.

Challenges and Considerations to Alignment

Speed Only Reduces Our Risks If
We Are Responding Nimbly to Feedback

Speed is only an advantage if we're moving in the correct direction. There's no value in quickly arriving at the wrong place. To avoid this, we need to incorporate actual, real feedback into our processes to ensure we are aligned at every step.

It is tempting to believe you are close enough to the exemplar of the user you're building for that you don't need outside inputs. "Don't I use software? Don't I understand this problem space?" you ask yourself. Yes, you do, and yet you have the curse of knowledge. You know what you meant to do, and you frame the questions in ways that work with the answers you already have, whether you mean to or not.

You must get true feedback in order to build the right thing for the right person quickly. Figure 6.4 shows a hierarchical view of the different types of feedback arranged in a pyramid to inspire us all to reach toward illumination.

Feedback Is Explicit (Surveys, Purchases)

Explicit feedback is the easiest to collect and trust. Are people buying? Are they telling you their net promoter score (NPS) is good? Ask your users directly how they feel about using your product and whether it works for their needs. This is the bottom layer of the feedback pyramid. You must have it before you can do anything. And though it's necessary, it is not sufficient.

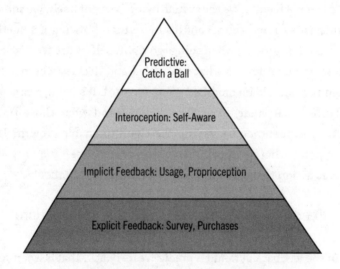

FIGURE 6.4: Feedback Pyramid

Feedback Is Implicit (Usage/Proprioception)

The next layer of feedback is implicit. To get this feedback, you must build a version of your software and allow people to use it. You must observe users interacting with your creation. After all, there is always a gap between what people say they do and what they actually do. It is the nature of humans to estimate these things poorly. So, you need some data on what it is people are actually doing, how they are using your software and product, what features aren't getting used, and so on. Maybe it's because it's not a helpful feature, or maybe it's just not something people know about or run across. This is like heat maps on web pages or informal paths on a grassy college campus. Not what people *should* do, but what they *actually* do.

This level of information seems straightforward, but it is extremely useful to have a professional with marketing or psychology experience to ensure that your questions are well-designed and give you meaningful data.

Feedback Is Self-Aware (Interoception)

The third layer of feedback is the system being aware of itself. We sometimes frame this as "system health," but it's more than noticing if something is going wrong; it's noticing when things go right. Self-aware feedback means a monitoring node notices what has scaled and decides whether that's a threshold that should be modified going forward. It's being aware of what you balance, what trade-offs you're making, and what those trade-offs serve. Are you spending heavily on the cloud to enable growth? Is there a tipping point where you will switch to maintenance? The observability data drives action through automated responses and runbooks.

Feedback Is Predictive (Accurate Anticipation)

The tip of the feedback pyramid is predictive feedback. That is when you have all the other layers, and you can afford to guess at what users want and check to see if your guesses are correct. Predictive feedback moves your product forward at the same time it iterates on what your users want and expect. It's last on the pyramid because bad predictions can be very dangerous for your user experience and reputation. In the best case, bad predictions are just wasted effort and lost opportunity cost. You don't want to do it until you are sure that you understand the constraints of the system in other ways.

Progressive Delivery relies on using the feedback from all four layers to ensure that you are delivering what users need, when they need it, at the least cost and risk to everyone.

Getting Started with Alignment

For Progressive Delivery to be effective, autonomy requires alignment. Where autonomy is tactical, alignment is strategic. Both are necessary, and together they build on each other. Alignment is not simply agreeing to the goals of the people in power. Alignment includes the state and direction of our teams, our dependencies, our constraints, and most of all, our users.

Evaluating for Alignment

When building a strategy for aligning constituents within your organization, here are some questions you can use.

First, here are questions that can be asked within your organization:

- What are your goals?
- Have these goals been accurately communicated to all stakeholders, constituents, and people who can make them happen?
- Who are all the stakeholders who should be included?
- Who is a part of the software delivery life cycle?
  - » Who is involved with strategy and ideation?
  - » Who is involved in the building?
  - » Who is involved with delivering?
  - » Who is involved with maintaining and providing feedback?
  - » Who is involved with incorporating that feedback?
- Do these people have the resources and autonomy necessary to do their part?
- Do any of these people have feedback or critical insights?

- Does what you are producing work with itself as well as other parts of your product?
- Is what you created accomplishing what you intended it to?
- How do you measure progress toward success? What performance metrics will tell you that you have done what you set out to do?
- How are people actually using your product? How do you know?
- How do you measure user happiness? (For example: Did the user use the feature? Could the user complete the task? Are users submitting help desk tickets?)
- Are you including explicit and implicit data in your feedback systems?
- Do you feel engaged?
- Do you understand what the company is doing?
- Do you feel like you have a voice?
- Do you feel you can work the way you want, in your environment, or at your hours?
- How do you align with your team?
- Do you feel like what you're making is good?
- How are you defining "good"?

Here are questions that can be asked of customers, partners, or other groups outside of your organization:

- Do they feel like the company will be here for a while? Is the organization trustworthy as a partner?
- Is the company configured in a way that fits in its ecosystem (software and world)? Is it extractive, exploitive, or innovative?
- Does it feel like the company understands its business needs?
- Is it easy to communicate with the company?

Tools and Practices That Enable Alignment

When thinking about alignment, the central theme is shared knowledge. There are performance measuring frameworks that help organize shared goals, and then there are communication tools. As you consider how information sharing fits within your organization's culture, here are some popular tools and practices to consider:

Systems tools and DevOps practices:
- monitoring and observability practices and platforms
- site reliability engineering (SRE)
- feature management platform (such as LaunchDarkly or Harness)
- CI/CD platforms
- test automation
- low code/no code

Communication tools:
- Slack
- Microsoft Teams
- email
- the watercooler

Work-tracking tools:
- Jira
- Asana
- Trello
- ServiceNow

Product tools:
- WalkMe
- Pendo
- Amplitude

Marketing tools:
- Google Analytics
- Pardot
- Marketo
- Adobe Experience Cloud

Performance and incentive tools:
- goal making/tracking culture
- key performance indicators (KPIs)
- objectives and key results (OKRs)

Conclusion

Alignment is the frame of reference through which our team, project, product, or company views the user and their world. Throughout this chapter, we've explored how alignment transforms the potentially jarring forces of abundance and autonomy into coordinated motion that delivers value to both software creators and users.

In the early days of computing, alignment was imposed from above through rigid specifications and command structures. Today's complex, distributed systems require a more sophisticated approach—one that establishes boundaries and interfaces rather than dictating every detail. This evolution mirrors our journey from monolithic releases to Progressive Delivery, where alignment extends beyond the development team to include the full spectrum of constituents in our software ecosystem.

Alignment in Progressive Delivery means understanding what users truly need (not just what they ask for), knowing when they need it (recognizing their readiness for change), and delivering it at the least cost and risk to everyone involved. It requires us to observe our systems holistically—not just the code and infrastructure, but the human systems that interact with our technology.

Feedback loops are essential to maintaining this alignment. By incorporating explicit feedback (what users tell us), implicit feedback (what their behavior shows), self-aware feedback (what our systems tell us), and ultimately predictive feedback (what we can anticipate), we create software that not only functions technically but genuinely serves its purpose in people's lives.

Alignment without abundance and autonomy is rigid and brittle—it stifles innovation and creativity. But abundance and autonomy without alignment create chaos—a series of technological jerks that may move quickly but never arrive at a destination. When properly balanced, these forces create a Progressive Delivery system that absorbs the shocks of rapid innovation while maintaining a clear direction toward creating value.

As you move forward in your Progressive Delivery journey, remember that alignment isn't about enforcing conformity or seeking unanimous agreement. It's about creating a shared understanding of where you're going and why, then allowing each person and component in your system to contribute their unique strengths toward that common destination. In Chapter 8, we'll explore how automation completes this framework, providing the consistent execution needed to operate at scale while preserving human creativity for the challenges that matter most. But next, we'll dive into a case study that better illustrates the importance of alignment in the context of Progressive Delivery.

Chapter 7

CASE STUDY: ADOBE

Alignment, when done well, enables even large teams and organizations to turn remarkably quickly and deliver incredible value.

Adobe is one of the world's most durable software brands. For decades, the Adobe suite of products has been the go-to tool for digital creatives, from large-scale companies to indie artists. As a company, Adobe has a long history of innovation, innovation that has aligned with the goal of allowing users of Adobe products to create personalized digital experiences.

Adobe has consistently sought to create a unified experience for users, whether they are using a single product or an entire suite of products, for a complete digital creative experience. A long-running example of this is the PDF. The portable document format (PDF) was initially released by Adobe in 1993 and is one of the most successful document formats ever created.

The PDF is also a great example of trust as a key part of the digital experience. A big part of the longevity and mass adoption of the PDF is that it renders consistently on all screens and systems that support the format. When you send a PDF to someone else, you know it will look identical to both you and the recipient. So, in a time when digital experiences are increasingly impacted by AI, Adobe had to work to maintain this goal of trust in the changing landscape of generative tools for creators.

Situation

In the early 2020s the landscape of creative design changed. OpenAI announced Dall-E, a text-to-image AI tool based on their GPT-3 model. With it, AI-based image generation suddenly captured the attention of the mainstream public. Adobe has been adding AI features in various products since 2016 with the Adobe AI platform Sensei. Sensei was originally a set of features incorporated into Adobe Premiere and Adobe Photoshop. As Adobe gained experience with machine learning (ML) and AI, it started to encourage the use of these technologies for internal use cases (such as support and code assistants) as well as incorporating them into products and features delivering customer value.

Complication

Even with Adobe's early work in ML and AI, they needed to find new ways to accelerate the release of enticing new technologies and rapidly expand the total addressable market of digital creators. Some users wanted new and exciting AI features; many other users needed their predictable, reliable Creative Suite to sustain their critical workflows. Adobe wanted to offer access and expertise. Amid all this, Adobe needed to be mindful and respectful of the creative licensing and legal needs and expectations of its core user base.

Question

The number of users who wanted to be hands-on with digital creation tools was rapidly expanding, but the needs and expectations of those users were simultaneously becoming more diverse. At the same time, Adobe had an established user base that was more interested in a stable and consistent user experience. How could Adobe provide the right users with the right experience at the right time?

Answer

Progressive Delivery enabled Adobe to deliver on the mainstream consumer expectations with the latest and most advanced image-based AI experiences while also maintaining a user experience and dialogue with their established user base. Legal considerations were clarified and made explicit. They maintained trust with their constituents—both users and the larger creative community—by preserving attribution and clarifying the sourcing of AI elements.

Why Alignment Matters

If one of your goals is to ensure users of your products trust your use of generative AI and the name of your flagship product is also a synonym for creative image manipulation—Photoshopping—you are likely going to take the time to make sure you get alignment right.

Adobe has been innovating with AI for a while and spends significant resources to ensure that users of their products can trust the outcomes that incorporate AI. Brian Scott, principal architect at Adobe, who spoke with us in 2024, said, "My legal and security teams are concerned about 'non-deterministic outcomes,' meaning we can't tell what the answer to a question will be until it's asked."[1]

The internal alignment needed for the teams across Adobe wasn't just on the product features and functionality, but on the broader context of how to manage AI technologies for the organization in general. Adobe's brand is synonymous with creative communities—the very communities that were most concerned and vocal about the use of unlicensed materials to train the popular public large language models (LLMs).

Alignment Strategy

First and foremost, Adobe wanted to ensure that it could properly assess the risk and impact using new AI tools. These tools could include a new LLM version, vendor, or AI product. Like many large companies, Adobe had a well-defined process for evaluating new vendors and products (like a collaboration product or new OSS package) when considering adopting new tools internally. Adobe was able to streamline this process to ensure all employees could make requests easily, and responses would be just as quick. As Brian Scott, one of the creators of this process, described it, "the process for a new LLM version is going to be different from a new vendor."

Adobe recognized that LLMs have different exposure levels depending on how they're used. A strictly internal enterprise LLM is trained on a known corpus, and the legal and security teams have full access and insight into what is going into and coming out of the model. The more customer-facing an LLM is, the less predictable it is, from both a legal and security perspective.

The key aspects that Adobe needed to design their process for were:

- Maintain customer and community trust.
- Continue to innovate to provide the tools and technologies that enable their users as well as internal teams.
- Accelerate the timeline for internal review and approval without compromising standards of quality and ethics.

Adobe recognized the technological jerk that AI was introducing for their product producers and consumers. It was clear the process would need to be updated to meet the needs of this accelerating rate of change.

These processes evolved as Adobe recognized the benefits of an abundance of resources that allowed for greater autonomy for their developers, allowing developers and teams to independently identify technologies that could accelerate and enhance their innovation.

What Changed

Before the technological jerk of AI, this process successfully enabled developers and teams to autonomously adopt tools and technologies. But AI presented two new challenges:

- rapid change coupled with material change of quality and value, and
- rapid change coupled with the risk of non-deterministic behavior.

The explosion of competition in the creation of LLMs was straining the established process. Before LLMs, the process had already been adapted to support SaaS products and services so that new versions or updates from existing vendors could be routed, evaluated, and approved quickly. Newer vendors would go through a lengthier process of legal and risk review to ensure both the products and the vendors met the legal and risk requirements that had been defined.

LLMs strained this process because of the rate of delivery and the drastic increase in performance coming with each new model from an increasing number of vendors. Evaluating and approving all these vendors and versions was further complicated by the inherent non-deterministic nature of LLMs and the increasingly questionable practices of some vendors. Many vendors were using unlicensed and copyrighted materials for their model training. Adobe had to carefully navigate how to deliver the right products to the right users at the right time.

By aligning with these objectives, Adobe was able to accelerate the pace of approval. "We're less resistant to onboarding new models, especially from a known vendor. We try to provide an SLA of approving models of one to two days, sometimes the approval can happen the same day," said Brian Scott. This enabled developers and teams to maintain their autonomy and move at the pace of innovation.

Progressive Release

Fortunately for Adobe, the requirement to progressively release the right products to the right users at the right time was initially addressed in their transition from packaged software to cloud-based application delivery. As Brian Scott pointed out, formerly, Adobe customers using "packaged" software expected this: "Adobe installations were deployed onto customer-run hardware. And so, the customer controls the rate of releases that we do. So, we'd see one customer maybe on a two- or three-year-old version for a certain reason, while the next customer will always want the latest release. Those versions are more controlled by the end user."

Since the company transitioned from selling packaged software to selling Creative Cloud subscriptions (the company's cloud-based application platform), "the end users have less control when they want to accept new versions," said Scott. "But, even with Creative Cloud, users can adjust the settings to control which applications get updated and when. Now there are cases where there's a major vulnerability, and we need to install this update. And we'll prompt the user to accept the update or accept the risk."

For Firefly (the Adobe image-based generative AI platform), Adobe has continued to offer this Progressive Delivery approach to incorporate new LLMs, allowing users to select the LLM they would like to use for a given request. "Firefly is released in major versions. So, version 1, version 2, version 3, etc. Right now in Firefly, you, as the end user, can say, I don't want to use version 3. I want to use version 1," explained Scott. This gives users the ability to maintain the use of a particular LLM version. This could be because they like the results better, or they're in the middle of a project and are trying to stick with a consistent model.

Adobe has many product teams, all operating semi-autonomously and deploying software as often as multiple times a day. To accommodate this autonomous delivery for multiple teams and products, Adobe uses a ring deployment technique, like the one illustrated in Figure 7.1. When software is deployed, it is first tested by the internal team and then by a larger team. An early release may be available to customers who have proactively indicated they want to see new or beta features and choose to have that particular feature active.

Only once all these gates have been successfully passed will a feature be available as part of a larger monthly release. In addition to opting into new features, users can opt out of new things, especially new AI models that may alter the work they have in progress.

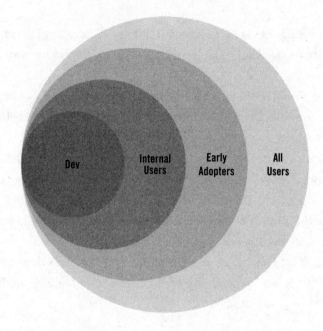

FIGURE 7.1: Ring Deployment

The practice of exposing software to an increasingly larger audience.

This is also a good example of the way Adobe separates deployment from the release of code. In the case of LLMs, Adobe wants its developers to iterate as quickly as they want to drive innovation and rapid product development. But Adobe has a feature management platform to manage the progressive release of code and LLM versions to its users. "Because these versions are actually iterating very quickly, we want to have some form of version pinning. We want to fix a particular model, but we also want teams to move as fast as they want," said Scott.

Adoption Autonomy

When internal Adobe teams propose onboarding new technology, they use a technology radar system to show the requesting team how their solution compares to existing tools the company has already built or licensed. "When adopting AI models, we still use this process, but the comparison points are about performance and quality for users, not just whether we have something that is mostly similar. We try to have a standard of quick response to requests for models because we know they move very quickly," said Scott.

Adobe Creative Cloud has different impacts than Adobe Experience Manager, for example, and understanding the business needs behind each allows Adobe to shape the way deployment works for them. In Creative Cloud, teams can iterate versions at the speed that works for them within the support windows. However, Experience Manager is often installed on customer-operated hardware. In that case, a customer may rightfully want to control the number and speed of releases. Those users have more control over their adoption speed.

"The rate of change for version pinning and releases depends on the product, but it also depends on whether the software is cloud-based or installed locally," explained Scott.

Cadence Not Stagnation

User choice is not intended to be a liability. This is where the alignment strategy needs to consider what the appropriate user cadence is and how that cadence gets support from the company or product end-of-life (EOL) policy. As Scott pointed out, "Obviously, at some point, we're going to phase out version 1 [of Firefly]. As models get more efficient, they use less power and put less pressure on the production stack." However, Adobe strives to incorporate the needs of the user into this process. "We obviously don't want to give folks access to all our models for too long. But I think that goes with any piece of software. There's some point where you have to have an EOL policy."

End of Life

In Figure 7.2, we show the inverse of ring deployment, the end-of-life cycle, where software is phased out of use or user access. As we will discuss in Chapter 10, the life cycle of software does not end when it is generally released. Instead, it becomes less and less supported and harder to access and install. Planning for that side of usage is a crucial part of how Adobe ensures that its customers do not experience painful jerks in their workflow.

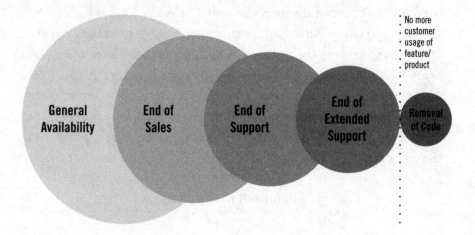

FIGURE 7.2: Software End-of-Life Diagram

Different organizations and different people have varying rates of acceptance of change. Adobe is thinking about this in relation to its analytics tool. The analytics tracking code needs to be embedded in customer pages, and updating it may be tricky or risky. Customers request the ability to have very long lifetimes on their versions because not all pages are so fluid that they get updated monthly. The end customers need the stability of knowing exactly how the code embedded in their page will work now and will continue to work for years. Thus, Adobe needs to consider both downstream and upstream dependency mapping. There's a point of congestion where the provider needs to stop supporting a version, but they can't because there's a chain of customers with downstream dependencies.

Adobe manages end of life at scale by making sure everything it supports will still be supported in new versions. Updates providing new features and functions must ensure that they do not break old ones. "It's not always possible to completely avoid breaking changes, but we can try to be transparent about what is more and less stable. One of the things we don't know yet is how long AI models that we didn't create and are currently licensing will be available. We can control the lifespan of our own models, to a degree, but keeping all of them forever will be pretty expensive," said Scott.

Progressive Delivery allows organizations to build more informed approaches to end-of-life transitions, by leveraging feature flags for product and feature sunsetting. By wrapping the code to be removed in a feature flag, access to the feature can be slowly removed from users who are not actively using it, and users and accounts that are still using the feature can be contacted to offer assistance in migration or reminders to move to the replacement workflow. Once usage has dropped to zero, the code can be safely removed from the code base without fear of failure to the overall product or service.

Alignment in Practice

Adobe is a great example of Progressive Delivery as a holistic software development life cycle. It starts from product ideation and development, incorporating a modern approach by adopting OSS software, aggressively deploying code to production, progressive releasing to an expanding user base through ring deployments, radical delegation of adoption cadence to end users, and leveraging observability and product analytics to end-of-life features.

Alignment was driven by the adaptation the company made because of the emergence of generative AI technologies. However, the need for increased alignment is not about AI specifically, but rather the technological jerk caused by an increase in the rate of acceleration. Fortunately, because Adobe already practiced a Progressive Delivery approach, they continue to support user needs around release cadence and developer desires around innovation.

Summary

The Adobe case study touches on many of the questions we asked in the last chapter:

- Who are all the stakeholders who should be included?
- Who is a part of the software delivery life cycle?
- Do these people have the resources and autonomy necessary to do their part?
- Do any of these people have feedback or critical insights?
- Do you include explicit and implicit data in your feedback systems?

Alignment represents a critical element in balancing technological innovation with user expectations. By aligning their strategic approach to AI adoption with both business objectives and customer needs, Adobe demonstrates how Progressive Delivery eases the technological jerk of emerging technologies. The key lies not in restraining innovation, but in creating thoughtful frameworks that maintain user trust while enabling exploration of new capabilities.

For Adobe, this alignment with the users' needs for controlled rollouts of new models (allowing the user to choose the model version they desire) required the business to implement new processes. However, instead of implementing processes that would restrict the speed and autonomy of developers, the organization was able to increase the speed of innovation and experimentation for those building features and products. The control point for adoption was delegated to the users as a way to allow the user to choose their own cadence of change. This control helps to smooth out the abrupt jerks of technological change.

The journey toward true alignment required Adobe to develop sophisticated, nuanced approaches to technology adoption. Tools like feature management, ring deployments, and version pinning facilitated this transformation, allowing Adobe to deploy cutting-edge AI capabilities while giving users control over their adoption pace. As demonstrated by Adobe's approach to Firefly and Creative Cloud, successful alignment isn't about imposing a single timeline on all users, but about creating intelligent systems that respect different user needs while maintaining forward momentum.

Adobe's example illustrates the power of Progressive Delivery as a holistic approach to software development. From ideation through development, deployment, release, and end-of-life management, alignment principles guided their decision-making. By separating deployment from release and empowering users with choice, Adobe successfully balanced competing demands of innovation speed and user readiness—delivering the right feature to the right users at the right time while preserving the trust that forms the foundation of their relationship with creative communities worldwide.

Chapter 8

AUTOMATION

The final test of fatigue elimination, as of every other change made in doing things, is its influence upon the total output of "Happiness Minutes." The aim of life is happiness, no matter how we differ as to what true happiness means. Have you reason to believe that your workers are really happier because of the work that you have done on fatigue study? Do they look happier, and say they are happier? Then your fatigue eliminating work has been worthwhile in the highest sense of the term, no matter what the financial outcome.

—**Frank and Lillian Gilbreth**, *Fatigue Studies*, 1916

In physics, jerk is the sudden, unexpected change in acceleration that throws us off balance. As we have applied this to our four A's, abundance is our technological potential energy, autonomy our force vectors, and alignment provides a frame of reference. In this metaphoric construct, automation is our spring constant (or shock absorber). This is the stabilizing force that transforms erratic motion into smooth, predictable progress. Just as modern vehicles use sophisticated computerized systems to dampen vibrations, monitor performance, and apply corrections without driver intervention, automation in software development absorbs the technological jerks that would otherwise ripple through our systems and disrupt our users.

The paradox of technological motion is that as our systems accelerate, manual intervention becomes both more necessary and less feasible. No human hand could possibly react quickly enough to the cascading changes in a complex distributed system. Automation becomes not just a convenience but a physical necessity—the only force capable of responding at the speed our technological pace requires.

Thus far, we've explored abundance, autonomy, and alignment. It means having the resources necessary to build without restriction, the freedom to innovate, and the shared vision that keeps us on track in a rapidly changing environment. So, how do we take this a step further and continue to innovate, build, and deliver as the rate of change continues to increase? Automation—the technology that transforms jerky, unpredictable motion into smooth Progressive Delivery.

au·to·ma·tion (ôdə'mäSH(ə)n, 'ädə'mäSH(ə)n): Identification and implementation of programmatic processes to repetitive tasks.

Automation allows you to operate at the scale and pace your stakeholders need and want. It reduces toil and creates stability and reliability. It establishes and maintains trust. Without automation, you're working in a non-reproducible manner and (very likely) wasting effort. But it's important to remember that automation without alignment is also wasted energy and can lead to chaos. An automated email campaign with broken personalization or one that looks like spam will cause a recipient to trust you less than not emailing at all.

Automation often brings up Jetsons-like images of a robot that performs functions for you, like an anthropomorphic housekeeper in a frilly apron or a machine that does your hair and makeup in a flash. But in reality, it looks more like a shopping website, a QR code, a delivery driver, or a work ticket. We're not replacing work via automation; we're redistributing it.

A very tiny percentage of "tech people" write machine language. They have created an automation chain that everyone further up the stack relies on. We don't have to think much about how to talk to a chip, or even our operating systems. In turn, there are people further up the stack who don't think about the work you do.

Automation is not magic; it's just a different, sometimes more efficient, way to do the same work. When Google predicts the next couple of words of a sentence when you're writing an email, it's not generating that out of nothing; it's basing it on the millions and millions of emails that it has processed. Nothing comes from nothing. Automation comes from experience.

For Progressive Delivery, automation is the second of the two ways to focus abundance and autonomy. Automation strengthens alignment and adds constraints by intentionally looking for repetitive manual tasks and creating code to reduce the effort required for such repetition. This also ensures consistency in the execution of such tasks so the user experience is deterministic and predictable. DevOps often refers to these manual tasks as toil. In the context of user experience, this can also be a common example of "paper-cut issues" (minor, yet frustrating, problems or imperfections in a product or system).

When we discuss automation as part of Progressive Delivery, remember that we can't automate what we don't understand. This is why automation is coupled with alignment. We don't need to know every bit or commit by heart, but we do need to know what we want included, at least by class, and what we want for outcomes. We need to understand enough of what we're building to be sure that our automation is what it needs to be.

Measuring automation can be done both directly and indirectly. Direct measurement can be done by using observability tooling to examine the frequency of pattern repetition as users navigate a workflow or end-to-end task. Indirectly, user surveys and interviews can target questions about repetition and "too many steps" to accomplish frequent tasks.

Historical Context of Automation

As computers became a standard part of the workplace, managing them became a dedicated job, then an entire department. One of the many reasons Y2K mitigations took so much work was that many of the systems that needed to be updated required direct physical interaction. Each desktop computer required the same set of steps, often for multiple pieces of software. That's a lot of manual work.

PXE (preboot execution environment, pronounced "pixie") was released in September of 1999. It was an automation tool that allowed administrators to push out updates to networked computers from a single server. Other administration tools predated it, but it was the first to gain wide adoption in the enterprise. Now, instead of dozens of IT workers trying to update computers physically after working hours, or trying to walk end users through a complicated process, a single image could be distributed to computers on the internal network.

This change increased the capacity of every administrator. This kind of force multiplication is evident in the AWS case study as well (see Chapter 9). Adding the ability to perform routine tasks automatically reduces work for everyone—allowing users and builders to focus on more complicated and creative tasks—and allows teams to manage a greater workload.

Abundance requires automation to capitalize on the full potential of limitless resources. When we were still working at a scale where we could FTP files to a server to update a web page, we didn't need it. It was only after we reached a point where the online space became so enormous that we needed automation in order to maintain our sanity.

Key Principles and Applications

What Makes Automation Useful:
Move from Explore to Bore

One of the most charming things about old-school sysadmins and their spiritual descendants, the SRE team, is their hatred of surprises. Their goal for a system is that no one has to think about it. That's the true definition of a platform, right? The thing you use to do your work and never think about whether it is working or not.

Developers are explorers. They crave novelty. They want to push the boundaries, learn new things, put things together in novel ways. They are tolerant of mistakes because most of the things they're doing aren't load-bearing or business-critical yet.

When something moves from "nifty" to boring, when it becomes main-tenance instead of invention, that's when automation is useful. The paths have been charted, and now they need to be widened and paved. Once it's known, it can be automated, boring, or table stakes. But to get to that place, we need to blaze the trail and understand the destination.

Automation Solves Problems Its Own Way

Automation depends on us to define where we want it to go or avoid going. When scientists were experimenting with slime molds to draw efficient transit networks, they put food at major city nodes and made bodies of water off-limits. The slime mold was able to understand those constraints and work around them, creating a perfectly usable transit map.[1]

If we say that content moderation should ban or hide certain words, we don't reduce those sentiments; we get a bunch of people and machines working around the ban and saying things like "unalive" instead of "dead." That's because automation is doing exactly what we told it to do: ban a specific word.

Automation needs abundance, autonomy, and alignment to work well. We can't make rules for execution if we don't have the resources to enforce or encourage them. We can't be consistent if we don't have a way to let the system and its parts act and react. Our rules are far less useful if we're not aligned on the system's goals and outcomes. When we construct automation, we're building on all the parts of the system that we've already discussed.

Progressive Delivery is iterative, not linear. Once you automate something, you may find a way your system can have more autonomy, so you rework it. Automation depends on previous A's, not because it's the final or win stage of Progressive Delivery, but because your software is never finished.

Wardley's Explorer/Villager/Town Planner

Simon Wardley described software discovery and creation as a series of roles. First, the explorer adventures into a space unknown (to them) and determines the value and opportunity. Then the villager starts to make a life in the new place, according to what they individually need. Finally, when enough people are "living" in an area, a town planner rationalizes and optimizes the way everything works together to create efficiencies of scale and effort.

In this model, it's easy to think of just the town planner as automation, but all three roles are needed for automation. You can't automate something that is terra incognita; it must be explored and mapped. You can't automate something that is only mapped but not experienced; it must have sufficient use to show patterns. Only when something is both useful and used is it worth automating. All of us have probably experienced enough premature optimization to know this, if we remember to apply our hard lessons.

If you want to automate a software build process, it might seem attractive to just set it up fresh and clean and the right way, but if you do that, you won't capture the way the team is actually building software. Instead, waiting and observing how they build and release software will show you what parts are needed, like automated integration testing, and what parts are currently irrelevant, like an SBOM.

Is Automation Working for You?

The perpetual promise and dream of automation is that it will save us time and effort. However, Jevons paradox reveals an interesting contradiction: As we make something more efficient or cheaper, usage typically increases. You've likely experienced this yourself. Consider the difference between paying per character in a text message versus having unlimited texting. When the cost of sending text messages dropped, the volume and length of our messages dramatically increased.

Despite this, we continue to believe that automation reduces effort. One key reason is that many of our automations *hide* complexity rather than *eliminate* it. Automation creates abstraction layers that shield us from underlying intricacies. Software developer Julia Evans described this when she asked what happens when you press a key in your terminal. Behind that seemingly simple action lies a complex chain of escape sequences, terminal encoding, echoing, and newlines. And that's just how the information is transmitted, not even how it's processed.[2]

This abstraction provides tremendous benefits. When you type "ls," you don't need to consciously think about the file system architecture—

you simply expect to see a list of files in your current directory. Automation frees your mental bandwidth by handling these complexities invisibly, though they still exist beneath the surface.

At its best, automation provides elegant solutions that transcend the simple replication of human effort. Consider trying to calculate the volume of a complex three-dimensional shape, like an ornate Bundt cake pan. You could attempt to measure every curve and angle mathematically, an enormously complicated task. Or you could simply fill the pan with water and then measure the volume of water. In this analogy, the water is automation: It conforms perfectly to the problem space, providing a solution that's fundamentally different from how humans would manually approach the task.

Similarly, digital drawing tools demonstrate this principle well. Creating a perfect circle and filling it with perfectly even color is surprisingly difficult for humans to do manually, but trivial with software. The computer doesn't just perform these tasks faster—it performs them in a fundamentally different way that produces better results with less effort.

The most valuable automation isn't just about reproducing human work and making it faster; it's about transforming how work gets done. Like water in a Bundt cake pan or slime mold finding the perfect path through complex terrain, effective automation follows the contours of problems in ways human processes cannot.

Benefits

What We Automate

Automation is a force multiplier for human work. When we automate a task, we are trying to make the task easier or more efficient for the person running the automation. Automating a task makes it a stable platform that we can use to do more advanced or creative work. We automate work that falls into the following categories:

Work We Value but Don't Enjoy

There are lots of things that need to be done, but doing them is tedious, or physically stressful, or just not enjoyable. When we can, we offload this work to machines, like laundry and dish washing. We want it done, but we don't want to do it.

Frequently, low-paid labor is an intermediate step in this automation. Food harvesting is an excellent example of this. There are some foods that we harvest automatically, like wheat and corn and even oranges. For other foods, it is still cheaper for the producer to pay humans to harvest them, like asparagus or apples. Sometimes this is because the food is fragile or hard to harvest in some other way. However, as wages rise, it becomes more economical and reasonable to invent and run machines that can do the work.

In a technological sense, we try to automate anything that we can describe well, because the act of description is very close to the act of automation. Setting out to build automation for something we've never done before is an exercise in frustration (or iteration, depending on your optimism). How can you write procedural steps for something if you haven't discovered the steps? How can you optimize something undefined? Even if it's work we don't enjoy, we need to do it a few times to understand what we're automating.

Work That Needs To Be Very Precise

Everyone cares about banking transactions being accurate because it involves money, which is the easiest way to describe value. Thus, banks are motivated not to lose track of even fractions of percentages, and people are motivated to be sure they keep all the money they have earned. Humans, even the most accurate humans, don't always do things exactly right. So, we have automated things like calculation and transfer, because it must be precise. Money is also easy, because unlike, say, a spleen, it has a very clear definition and form.

We also don't hand-draw circuits anymore. We use software to help us design and etch the chips that everyone counts on every day. By applying the efforts of many people to make an automation as perfect as possible, we end up with an automation that we can treat as finished and more accurate than any single human.

Things That Are Complex

We automate things that are complex. This seems counterintuitive—because it's difficult to describe complexity accurately—but it's one of the only ways we can manage the very large abilities we've gained from abundance. No single human is picking out the ads you see in your social media feed. Instead, they are the result of data aggregation and analysis that identifies you as part of a demographic, ad buyers choosing to target your demographic, and ad bidding houses that require milliseconds of response time to load the ad on your page as it's rendering. The act of assembling the "front page" of any given news site is orders of magnitude more complicated than when newspapers ran printed paper through a waxing machine to do manual paste-up, which in turn was much more complicated than setting text in a movable type printer.

Work That Crosses Domains

We automate work that crosses boundaries between different systems, teams, or phases. Think of a relay race, where the most critical—and risky—moments occur during the handoff of the baton between runners. Each runner might be exceptionally fast, but if the handoff is fumbled, the entire race is compromised. Similarly, our workflows often falter not within specialized domains but at the transitions between them.

Consider the journey of information through a healthcare system. A patient's test results might be processed efficiently in the lab but then sit in an electronic queue waiting for a nurse to review them, then wait again for a doctor's interpretation, and finally languish until someone communicates the findings to the patient. The actual analysis might take minutes, but the entire process could stretch into days because of these handoff delays.

Automation functions as the perfect relay runner who never drops the baton. When a test result is completed, automated systems can immediately route it to the appropriate medical professional, trigger notifications, schedule follow-up appointments, and update patient records—all without the information sitting idle at domain boundaries. Each specialized team can still apply its expertise, but the transitions between them become seamless rather than friction points.

Bug tracking systems exemplify this principle in software development. Finding the bug, reporting it, fixing it, verifying the solution, and documenting the change may all happen in different domains with different specialists. Automation ensures the information flows continuously across these boundaries, maintaining momentum instead of getting trapped in organizational silos or communication gaps.

Challenges and Considerations

Work That's Hard to Automate

Even as automation transforms countless aspects of our world, certain categories of work remain stubbornly resistant to automation. Understanding why these types of work are difficult to automate helps us make better decisions about where to focus our automation efforts and where the human touch remains essential.

The difficulty in automating certain work (what we might call "hard" work) stems from several fundamental challenges. First, work that is hard to automate often defies clear definition or standardization. Automation requires well-defined parameters, explicit rules, and predictable environments, but human activities often thrive in ambiguity and exception handling. Second, work that requires genuine understanding rather than pattern matching remains challenging to automate. While AI systems can mimic understanding within narrow domains, they lack the contextual intelligence and embodied experience that humans bring to complex situations. Finally, work involving genuine creativity, empathy, or ethical judgment exists in domains where automation may augment but cannot replace human involvement.

We keep attempting to capture the algorithms that make us human—to formalize intuition, creativity, and wisdom into programmable steps—

but these efforts reveal both the impressive progress of automation and its inherent limitations. This isn't to diminish automation's potential, but rather to help us appreciate where human contribution remains irreplaceable, even as we continue trying to eliminate unnecessary toil. Let's explore some of these challenging areas:

Creative Work

As we write this book, there has been an explosion in publicly available AI engines like Midjourney and ChatGPT. As is always true for new technologies, the advocates claim that a technology is world-changing and the skeptics declare that it's bunk. The reality is that AI is useful for the things it's good at, and not yet as useful as the hype merchants promise it will be.

What we can't automate, even if we can simulate and remix things, is originality, creativity, and leaps in logic. We can train a computer in what most people find beautiful, and it can remix the elements of beauty into something we find beautiful, but the computer itself cannot perceive beauty. It's just following the prompts and corpus that the designers have designated as likely to cause beauty.

As much as we've tried, we can't automate inspiration. We have trouble teaching systems to think in systems, and although there are some interesting things happening in very narrow areas of creativity, like chess and Go, automation is not very good at useful novelty or creativity. It's really good at trying all the existing combinations of something. Protein folding is something humans can't do at scale, or fast, but computers can. Thank you, computers, for not dying of boredom while you alter a molecule one bond at a time.

Care Work

It's really hard to automate the human/machine interface, as anyone who has ever dealt with a phone tree knows. Humans are extremely variable, and machines and computers lack the flexibility of thought and analogy to handle that. Instead, humans learn a specific syntax and method of interacting with a machine interface. I bet you can identify the human side of a phone tree/automated conversation when you hear it, because the person talking isn't speaking their own language, they are speaking the Machinglish version of it. Learning Machinglish is a life skill, and we don't even notice we're doing it.

That mostly works for humans who understand the machine's goals and want to cooperate with it. However, that's a distinct subset of humanity. We haven't been able to automate care work, as desperately as we wish we could, because our machines aren't smart enough and because people don't thrive in this situation.

If you tried to create a diaper-changing robot, the baby would absolutely end up on the floor, because part of changing a diaper is being alert for the sudden lurch toward the edge of a changing table, part of it is cleaning up something sticky, part of it is making the process not emotionally traumatic, part of it is getting the fastenings right by feel, and all of what you learn about one baby in one week may be entirely different the next week. There isn't an algorithm that can handle that, yet.

We also know that care work is physically and mentally exhausting, but that having an emotional connection between the caregiver and care recipient is important to everyone's emotional health.[3] When we try to create a caretaking robot, the first thing we do is try to endow it with friendliness, not a comprehensive understanding of the UV changes in skin that presage a bedsore (although, that would be useful).

During the COVID-19 pandemic lock downs, many of us learned concepts like skin hunger and the difference between in-person and televisual communication. Automating around that is a really high bar, and although some organizations are trying for it, automation of loving kindness is a long way from where we are.

Work We Don't Understand

We can't automate what we don't understand. Doing something manually is always an essential part of automating a process, and sometimes it's hard for us to see all the parts and elements of a process that we want to automate. Think of the common technical writing test: "Write the instructions for making a peanut butter and jelly sandwich." If we tell a human to "take a couple of pieces of bread," we can rely on a lot of preexisting patterns and common sense. Your average human knows that "a couple of pieces" means two. They'll also know that they have to open the bread bag first and how to get past the tab or tie at the mouth of the bag, and they will generally not take the heel of bread for a sandwich. All of that is something we would have to explain if we were automating making a PB&J. But sandwiches are trivially complex compared to some of the things we automate, like continuous integration. CI doesn't end up with jammy knives on the kitchen counter, though, so there's that.

Any automation is usually an approximation to start with: We automate the parts we know and understand and then wait to see what breaks so we can find the parts we didn't know about or understand before automation. But an automation is never fully finished because something will almost always change, eventually. Even automations we think of as very mature, like those car-welding robots we see in automotive factories, need to be reprogrammable. There will be new body models or different makes of cars.

If we have to understand something to automate it, and if the automation is always going to change, does it really make sense to automate it? Well, yes, because we don't want to do it. Because the act of automating has taught us more about the process. And because even if we have to change some parts of the script, most of it stays intact.

Automation is not so much "set and forget" as it is Mickey's broom in "The Sorcerer's Apprentice" scene of Disney's *Fantasia*. It will save us work, but only if we are sure we have set boundaries, limits, and expectations. Without that, we might find ourselves like the apprentice, desperately trying to stop an automation that has multiplied beyond our control and is now flooding our workshop.

When we seek to understand something so we can automate it, we learn about it in different ways than we would if we were going to teach it to a human. For instance, I would teach a human to knead bread by touch, but a bread machine does it by humidity and resistance and other senses that are foreign to a human. There is always a layer between an expert who knows how to do something the human way and the translation for the machine way of doing that same thing. You can smell a peach and say,

"This is ripe." But you must tell a machine to use its sensors for ethylene, because the machine doesn't understand "ripe" until we tell it what the exemplar is.

We can't automate without exemplars, and we can't get to exemplars without experience, and experience requires getting it wrong a lot of times. And while it's easy to wish we could automate getting things wrong, so we didn't have to experience it, that's not how humans learn.

Getting Started with Automation

As we've laid out in this book, Progressive Delivery assumes you're already practicing continuous integration and continuous delivery. The mechanical parts of being a release manager have been automated away, leaving only the residual and difficult emotional labor parts. We have automated lots of the predictable testing, like unit-level and integration testing, leaving only the exciting parts where everything works fine except this one weird edge case. We have automated bug tracking, payments, workflows, authorization, and authentication. What we have left are mostly the interesting problems. And most of us like working on interesting problems more than rote, automatable problems.

Evaluating for Automation

Automation is not set it and forget it. It will always be a work in progress, and you will want to leave space for processes to be updated as the application evolves. Some questions to consider as you look for areas you can automate include:

- Is it easier to do this manually or automatically?
- Does it save time, money, or labor?
- Does automating this allow expertise to be redirected or shared?
- What data do I need to understand to describe the automation?
- How will I know if the automation needs to be changed?

- Is this automation reducing toil or joy?
- Are you doing toil?
- How often do you have to repeat tasks?
- How much can you share a task with a coworker?
- What is the state of your documentation, security, and compliance measures?
- Are you able to audit your work clearly?

Tools and Practices That Enable Automation

As you review your systems and think about which parts can be automated, here are some popular tools and processes to consider:

- monitoring and observability practices and platforms
- alerting systems
- feature flags that enable automatic operational changes
- low-code/no-code solutions that encourage abstraction
- templates, patterns, and tools that describe known solutions
- DevOps
- SRE
- platform engineering
- event-driven architecture
- infrastructure-as-code (IaC)

Conclusion

Throughout this journey through the four A's of Progressive Delivery, we've seen how each element builds upon and complements the others. Now that we have an abundance of resources, autonomy to act as needed, and alignment to help us stay focused, we arrive at automation—the stabilizing force that transforms erratic technological motion into smooth, predictable progress. Automation comes from experience and understanding, not from theoretical planning alone. It crystallizes the patterns we've observed, the processes we've refined, and the knowledge we've accumulated. Just as a skilled driver develops muscle memory that makes complex maneuvers feel effortless, automation embeds our operational wisdom into systems that can perform consistently at scales that would overwhelm human capacity.

We typically automate work that falls into distinct categories: tasks we value but don't enjoy (reducing toil), operations that require precision beyond human consistency, processes that involve complexity across multiple domains, and workflows that need to bridge gaps between different systems or teams. In each case, automation doesn't simply make work faster; it fundamentally transforms how work gets done, often solving problems in ways humans wouldn't approach them.

Successful automation depends critically on the foundation laid by the other three A's. Without abundance, we lack the resources to build robust automated systems. Without autonomy, we can't implement and refine automation effectively. Without alignment, our automated systems might operate efficiently but in conflicting directions. The four A's work together as a unified system—each amplifying the others when properly balanced.

At its best, automation creates stability, reliability, and consistency while establishing and maintaining trust between systems, teams, and users. It enables organizations to operate at scales and speeds that would be impossible through manual efforts alone. When done poorly, however, automation can accelerate mistakes, amplify misalignments, or create brittle systems that collapse under unexpected conditions. Automation without alignment is particularly dangerous—wasted energy that can lead to chaos rather than progress.

As we've seen throughout this book, Progressive Delivery isn't about implementing specific technologies or following rigid methodologies. It's about balancing these fundamental forces—abundance, autonomy, alignment, and automation—to create systems that can deliver the right capabilities to the right users at the right time. By thoughtfully applying these principles, we transform the potentially disruptive jerks of technological change into a smooth, controlled acceleration toward delivering value.

In the next chapter, we'll explore how AWS has applied automation at unprecedented scale, creating automated systems that enable incredible technological momentum while maintaining the reliability that their millions of customers depend on.

Chapter 9

CASE STUDY: AMAZON WEB SERVICES

Automation is the essential underpinning for modern datacenter infrastructure management. The scale at which AWS operates is unprecedented, and it would be impossible to reliably and sustainably keep the lights on without sophisticated automation and processes in place. Amazon was already running the world's biggest e-commerce infrastructure when it launched AWS in 2006 and was using service orientation extensively with the idea that any service used internally could also be exposed to an external customer. However, running your own systems is very different from allowing customers to run their workloads on your infrastructure. The primitives need to be more generic, which is a far harder engineering and management challenge. Amazon set out to automate anything that it sees as "undifferentiated heavy lifting," for its own needs, and in the case of AWS, for external customers.

Situation

The AWS engineering culture is laser-focused on minimizing the potential impact of disruptions to customers. The key approach is to avoid single points of failure by maintaining separate regions and availability zones (AZs). These AZs are separate, independent, and physically isolated from each other. Within these AZs are smaller isolated units as part of a cell-based infrastructure. Everything is isolated, which means that disruption is contained. At the scale it operates, any downtime would immediately cause problems for millions of its customers and potentially billions of its customers' customers. AWS rollouts truly are at a global scale, so it has established a set of practices and technologies designed to eliminate as many risks as possible.

While AWS is unique in the scale of its challenges, particularly in supporting a wide range of third-party services and workloads, the lessons it has learned over the years are relevant to any organization pursuing strategies for modern, safe, fast application and infrastructure delivery.

"For us, a deployment is not deploying a package to one piece of software, it's how many regions and availability zones do we have in the world? So, when we are deploying, our blast radius is exceptionally high. I think we are exceptionally paranoid about the fact that a deployment is not just one pipeline that is in one datacenter. It's a pipeline that's across many, many, many regions. And so that is always in the top of our mind, especially these days," said Deepak Singh, VP of AWS.[1]

Complication

AWS is the world's biggest cloud computing environment. At the time of this writing, the AWS cloud operates one hundred and seventeen availability zones, within thirty-seven launched regions around the world. It does business in over two hundred countries and territories.

In Amazon's case, abundance is an opportunity but also a massive challenge. AWS services run the gamut from storage, compute, and messaging and networking infrastructure to managed services for every kind of database, containers, developer tools, AI, IoT, serverless functions, and security services. Everything you need, or might need, to build and deploy modern applications at scale, both primitives and higher-level abstractions.

These services are built and managed independently by autonomous teams, which makes AWS highly productive—it can build and operate new services with enviable velocity. But that autonomy comes at a cost—it creates a potential alignment problem, associated with greater complexity. Different product groups make their own infrastructure and design decisions. Though obviously there are some common tools and approaches, and within some systems a relatively high degree of homogeneity. Hundreds of teams doing their own thing, with customer obsession as a mantra, leads to a lack of internal standardization. So, the question became: How can automation help with alignment in terms of a cultural shift?

Unlike companies such as Meta, Google, or Spotify, at AWS there is not a single, standardized set of internal platform services for building and deploying services that every developer and operator in the company uses. Alignment is therefore more of a challenge than at these other hyperscalers.

Question

When an organization is able to leverage abundance to enable autonomy of developers to fuel innovation, how do you get teams to work together effectively? In delivering on the promise of Progressive Delivery across autonomous teams, how do you get alignment without top-down platform mandates?

Answer

AWS has been on a long journey to increase the automation of pipelines and testing, which should resonate with any company building applications. It's easy to assume that AWS emerged fully fledged in its current incarnation as a state-of-the-art cloud infrastructure, but the truth is it has evolved, which means these lessons are relevant not just to a startup or an enterprise scale-up but also to a bank in Frankfurt or a telco in Tokyo.

At AWS, there was no grand strategy or document about an overall strategy for reducing risk, given that teams were more focused on enabling innovation. Building alignment, therefore, took an iterative approach. Alignment is a social problem; automation is a tool that creates stability, reliability, and consistency.

A group of people from different AWS teams would sit down regularly to review all of the postmortems for the previous month and try to identify practices that reduced downtime and improved operations. The company encouraged friendly competition among teams to adopt pipelines and ensured that the pipeline automation was a good enough experience that developers wanted to use it.

Automation as Aspiration

A central tenet of availability at AWS is that everything starts from the atomic unit (of engineering team autonomy)—the one-box. A "one-box" is the smallest unit of deployment—it might be one machine, an EC2 instance, or container—where AWS starts production deployments to minimize impact before progressively deploying more broadly. However, it's not just a developer machine. Engineering teams can route user traffic to it to see how it performs in isolation.

AWS must reliably scale beyond each one-box into deployments at a global scale, and automated pipelines are the means of getting there. The AWS philosophy is do lots of testing before production and then deploy to a small percentage of production workloads first, before progressively rolling out. Once that's done, engineering teams have more confidence in what they roll out to the rest of the estate. Furthermore, they can roll back to a previous state if necessary.

So, deployments start with an auto-scaling group of one that AWS applies to the load balancer. That goes in the pipeline before the rest of the bigger auto-scaling group. AWS has an approach it would describe as "scrappy"—a compliment at the company—which was enough to drastically reduce risk in a way that AWS could monitor and ensure that all teams across the company were doing it.

At that point, the organization had reached a decision. Once the company realized the approach definitely reduced risk, it became a matter of encouraging everyone to use it.

"Most of the time we try to automate, because unautomated sticks [disincentives] add a lot of friction and not everybody loves them," said Singh.

This adoption of automated pipelines came with a significant benefit. AWS previously had an organizational role, the release captain, tasked with coordinating the release of code changes for their team's services and shepherding them to production. Now, they're not necessary. Teams have tools to enable the deployment and testing of software in pre-production and production and to manage rollbacks according to policy.

It's a much more efficient system. CI/CD systems have become automated release captains, which is like freeing up an engineer for every team. And the processes have become standardized across the organization, leading to more consistent practices.

Automation as Alignment

As it became clear that automation was helping to reduce toil, improve efficiencies, promote a more reliable product, and reinforce alignment, AWS built a platform to standardize these practices. The platform scans all the pipelines it uses against a rules engine that can be applied at the company, VP, or organizational level, which then notifies engineering teams if they are out of compliance with established standards. If necessary, the automated platform will stop the pipeline, and the team will not be able to deploy until it has implemented one-boxes in the pipeline. Another example would be if a team were using an older, insecure version of a package. Then the pipeline would not progress. This is the stick—certain practices are crucial to deployment safety, so if you don't meet those practices, you don't get to deploy.

Another way AWS reinforces alignment with automation is by remaining aligned with its users' needs. Unlike organizations shipping apps, AWS doesn't consider specific user cohorts as it builds its core services. One-boxes are also used to discover and understand workload patterns. A request landing on a one-box is, in effect, random across whatever customer happens to be using that zone or that cell, which is probabilistically spread across all requests. Observability and metrics in one-boxes are about understanding the behavior of the system once a "random" workload is deployed on it. The "cohorts" are workloads or sets of requests rather than sets of named users or accounts.

"In terms of pipelines, it's very workloads-oriented. Customers are self-selecting into those boundaries. They're choosing the regions; they're choosing the zones that they go into. We don't really think about types of users in that way. We don't have a (specific named) canary set of users, for example. We get a little bit of a benefit there because it's all kinds of workloads; it's an even spread of the types of workloads that are coming through during deployments," said Clare Ligouri, principal software engineer at AWS.

Experimentation with named users is done at the private beta level for a new service. AWS doesn't run the kind of application experimentation that might use feature flags across user cohorts. "We famously have done some experiments you could argue in with GAs, and we realized it didn't hit the mark, and we had to go back to the drawing board. But that's life," said Singh.

New services can be run as a separate endpoint, so workload patterns can be understood there. That's where a named user might come in. What account did something that caused a spike in metrics? Because the service is already tested for resiliency and won't be rolled out to a larger customer base, that's life, rather than a matter of life and death.

Deployment of the service, though, is still a controlled process with rate limiting. According to Singh, "We obviously put in safety like any new service will launch in limits. Part of the reason again is safety. You're protecting the service and over time, you get more comfortable with workload patterns, and we get to understand where the edges are, and we start raising those limits."

"So even in pre-production," said Liguori, "we're running monitoring canaries at least every one to five minutes. And making sure that they are healthy in a pre-production environment before it goes to production. And then that continues out into every individual production environment. So, it kind of comes back to us segmenting the one production into so many different environments that each have their own monitoring canaries so that we're keeping a really close eye on how deployments are affecting things."

Summary

Though we focused on how AWS built and managed automated pipelines, it is interesting to note that this is also a story about alignment. AWS benefited from so much abundance that sprawl became a potential issue. To maintain their competitive edge, AWS encouraged developers to innovate freely, extending autonomy with little restraint. While this enabled teams to continue pushing new ideas forward, the lack of alignment began to prove problematic as the organization and its product offerings scaled.

It was through automation that AWS found alignment. This iterative process is based on the desire to provide stable, reliable systems that could grow with them. Through this process of automating low-level tasks, AWS is all about reducing toil, the undifferentiated heavy lifting. AWS has driven standardization and alignment across its product teams.

While AWS does not describe its practices using the term Progressive Delivery, the patterns it uses map closely to those laid out in this book. Their focus on reducing risk through incremental deployment, extensive testing, and automated safety controls embodies the core principles of delivering the right capabilities to the right systems at the right time. What makes their approach particularly noteworthy is how they achieved alignment not through top-down mandates but through creating automated systems that made the right way the easiest way to work.

By building pipelines that incorporated best practices, AWS teams naturally gravitated toward consistent approaches. The automation itself became a cultural force for alignment, transforming what could have been chaotic autonomy into coordinated innovation that preserves AWS's legendary reliability despite its massive scale and complexity.

Chapter 10
FUTURE PROOFING

We can grow up. We can leave the nest. We can fulfill the Destiny, make homes for ourselves among the stars, and become some combination of what we want to become and whatever our new environments challenge us to become.

—**Octavia E. Butler**, *Parable of the Talents*

We don't think anyone actually knows the future. But that doesn't mean we will stop trying to see what's next. Using a phone flashlight to illuminate the next few steps of a vast, lightless cavern is better than walking around in absolute darkness. Even if we can't see the future in its entirety, we can see our next few steps, and Progressive Delivery makes it easier to avoid walking into giant pits.

Throughout this book, we've explored how Progressive Delivery provides a framework for navigating technological change—delivering the right functionality to the right users at the right time. The four pillars we've established—abundance, autonomy, alignment, and automation—work together to create systems that can adapt to changing conditions without creating those jarring technological jerks that disrupt users and organizations alike.

Future proofing represents the natural extension of Progressive Delivery principles. While Progressive Delivery helps us manage current rates of change, future proofing applies this same thinking to anticipate and prepare for changes yet to come. By separating current functionality from future capability, we create space for tomorrow's possibilities without requiring perfect foresight.

The same Progressive Delivery pillars that help us deliver value today are essential for future proofing. Abundance provides the resources to build with tomorrow in mind. Autonomy enables adaptation where it's needed without system-wide disruption. Alignment keeps us focused on enduring user needs rather than transient technology trends. Automation creates the reliable foundation that makes safe evolution possible.

As we explore what it means to future proof our systems, remember that this exploration isn't about predicting every possible outcome. It's about creating flexible, extensible systems that can gracefully evolve as the needs of our users and organizations change—delivering the right capabilities to the right people at the right time, even as "right" keeps changing.

What Is Future Proofing?

Future proofing is thinking about our products existing in conditions we can't yet predict. Is our meeting software going to become a way to conduct classes and funerals? Is our public television going to replace public schools? Is our SMS-based social app going to become the de facto standard for emergency notifications? We don't know, but if we future proof well (and get lucky), we may get to see our software do things we never imagined when we initially designed it.

In order to future proof, we first need to establish the time horizon we're looking at. Is the timescale weeks, months, years, or even decades? The longer we need something to be relevant, the more we have to design it to be extensible. How much ability do people have to make changes? And is it just the creators, or is it also the community or product users who are empowered to make changes?

Think of HTML. Tim Berners-Lee wrote the standard in 1993. In the last thirty years, we have iterated on it, added things to it, and removed some things (RIP <marquee> tag). The odds are good that you heard about this book on an HTML-based site. We're writing it in an HTML-variant word processor. HTML's flexibility has allowed much of what you think of as modern technology to thrive. In 1993, streaming video ads sold on an advertising arbitrage website with millisecond response times were even stranger than the cyberpunk futures we were writing. But here we all are, because HTML had that extension capacity.

We're not all trying to write the next HTML. For one thing, the financial incentives aren't there. For a standard to be widely adopted, it has to be open, which seldom leads to the kind of financial return that investors are motivated by.

We are trying to create products that are useful to other people, that are sustainable, and that meet our existing constraints. When we future proof, we want something that can adapt to changing constraints, as we discussed in the chapter on abundance.

No matter how much planning and interviewing and predicting we do when we create our product, no product vision survives first contact with the user.

There are a few types of future proofing:

- **Feature work:** Building features compatible with future technologies or future user needs (such as support for a new load balancing service or database schema change to support a new user workflow).
- **Infrastructure scaling:** Planning and building components to support future infrastructure changes (such as code to allow auto-scaling during service spikes or work required for multi-site scaling).
- **Performance scaling:** Improving the performance of existing code (to make a process run faster or make a process consume fewer resources).
- **Data independence:** Ensuring that you can export your data and use it with different vendors. Sometimes your vendor becomes unavailable, and sometimes your business has different needs. Future proofing allows organizations to retain control of their assets.

Future Proofing and Delegation

Think about future proofing in the context of autonomy. Ideally, you're shifting the use and control of functionality as close to the consumer as possible. They're the ones who should make the real-time decision on whether or not a feature or capability is useful or necessary to them. Progressive Delivery's value proposition is to build the right thing for the right user at the right time. For the user, this means fewer technological jerks. For the builder, this means that the more control users have with our software, the more accurately we can deliver value and reduce waste.

Think about future proofing in the context of abundance and trust. If you have the resources available for each consumer to be in their own context, they don't have to spend energy thinking about how to make their workflows fit into other people's expectations. Their experience does not come at the cost of anyone else's ability to operate. And our own abundance means we can allow experimentation and variety in our offerings.

Autonomy extends to extensibility. Exposing our APIs means the people using our software can choose how to consume it. Maybe it's better for them when it's integrated with their daily tools, or with a different analysis engine, or controlled by a dance pad. We can't know! But we can make it possible by leaving as much extensibility and optionality as possible.

Users also deserve as much security autonomy as we can provide. They should be able to decide whether a résumé will be retained for multiple years or whether a dating profile should be searchable. Thinking about the future when we set data retention and exposure means that our users can be sure we are respecting their needs now and in the future.

Think about future proofing in the context of alignment. This is possibly the most challenging aspect, because how can we predict what will align with the needs of people in the future? We do this by making it possible for them to use our tool in ways that are modular and broken out from our current product flow. Stewart Butterfield is the most prominent example of this creative reuse, having twice started companies to make games and ending up with successful companies doing something entirely different (Slack and Flickr).

Think about future proofing in the context of automation. Your product's inclusion in automation depends on how easy it is to access programmatically. The more effort you put into making sure your inputs and outputs are standard, no matter what the user experience is, the more likely you are to be included in a toolchain of the future. The best kind of software is the kind that you never think about using because it's so much a part of your life. Getting there and staying there in the future means consumers have automated you into their process. Staying there happens only if your software is easy to upgrade and integrate.

Consumer Empowerment

If a consumer chooses to use something we made when they have other choices, it's a strong signal that what we offer them is valuable.

With larger features, control and customization may be served through paid access. Money exchanged for access to a feature is a direct indication of value. For smaller changes (or changes that are hidden from the user), the value is less directly traceable, but you can use feature flags, math, and statistics to determine whether or not new code is successful and should be rolled out to larger groups of users.

Consider the way Google launched Gmail and used statistics on the front end to determine who the power users were and then provide them with the option of upgrading to a new kind of user experience. Later, Google even delegated this control down to the individual user with the advanced "Labs'" settings. From these advanced settings, users could turn on and off whole features that were not part of the default experience. That was an early example of radical delegation to the end user.

Large social media companies regularly use a Progressive Delivery approach to expose small cohorts (typically power users) to new features or improvements in their service to gauge how changes will land with their broader user base. Sometimes this is a great way to advertise a new feature, and other times this is a great way to fail fast and course correct quickly.

Some of the challenges in feature delegation are knowing your user base, how sticky it is, and how tolerant it is of change. Knowing this will dictate what you can change. User tolerance also depends on your product use case, traction, maturity, and criticality.

For example, an enterprise security software company will not introduce a new login or authentication sequence to 1% of its power users without some preparation and notification prior to release. You may want to prime your early group to be excited about adoption or avoid shocking change-averse users. We can't tell you what emotions your users have. We just want to remind you that users feel things about their tools.

This calculation of factors is why *deployment* is about software getting where it needs to go, and *release* is about what the user experiences. Figure 10.1 provides a visual representation of how to think about the separation of deployment and release. In the diagram, we can see how the activities relate to who owns the activity and who is impacted by that portion of the cycle, as well as who participates in that particular feedback loop.

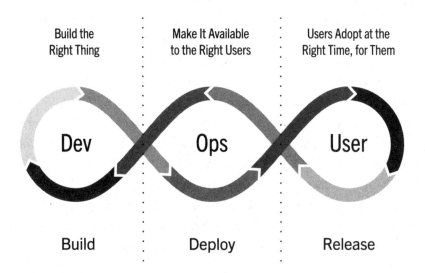

| Build the Right Thing | Make It Available to the Right Users | Users Adopt at the Right Time, for Them |

Dev — **Ops** — **User**

| Build | Deploy | Release |

FIGURE 10.1: Deployment vs. Release and Who's Impacted

We also need to be able to undo changes if and when we discover they are unwelcome. Building in a way that makes it fast and easy to reverse our releases is a part of making them safer to release. Feature flags are an elegant way to distribute code that can behave in different ways at runtime without needing to replace the whole code base exposed to the user end.

The best changes are often transparent to your audience. This doesn't mean you keep the look and feel of your GeoCities site from the late 1990s, but your users shouldn't have to do a Google search to figure out how to complete a task they do every day because your software drastically changed overnight.

One positive example of this is the user interface design of GitHub. GitHub makes hundreds of changes a month to things like text color, button placement, component size, and so on. However, for regular users, these changes are mostly imperceptible. With each change, GitHub tracks the user productivity associated with the affected workflows. If the outcome is positive, the change stays; if not, it is reverted, and GitHub tries something different. Over time, users see vast changes to the user experience and to the user interface, but in the day-to-day, they don't really notice. Smaller changes, but more frequently.

In future proofing your software, this gradual evolution is exactly the type of user experience that you want.* Your product and services depend on how your organization thinks about change. Incremental changes, when building software, should be small and additive over time. This was made popular with Agile. Waterfall development required a rewrite with every release. Remember, though, organizations have reasons for choosing their release cadence, and it's important that you understand what those reasons are before you try to speed the cadence up.

The recognized value of smaller changes is the ability to make more granular course corrections and reduce work that isn't relevant to users. Continuous delivery used this methodology to reduce work unit size change and made the unit of change even smaller. The other adjustment with continuous delivery was a greater willingness to move the target or goal of a feature based on new information.

In Agile, we talk about our North Star Metric as the thing we were all aligned on reaching or creating. Continuous delivery doesn't eliminate the idea of that alignment, but it is not a single metric; instead, it features multiple metrics and a greater focus on and incorporation of monitoring and observability.

Thanks to this broadening of metrics that matter, teams and organizations can make more real-time assessments about progress in the product

---

* Unless it isn't, and you want a big, dramatic, simultaneous release. It still takes Progressive Delivery to make that happen safely.

from both the perspective of the system and the user. This is a much tighter feedback loop because teams can deliver a unit of value much more quickly and see and measure the value.

Representation and Inclusivity Drive Value

Inclusivity and representation in the people building our products are essential parts of sound future proofing. It is so easy for technologists to make the things that we want ourselves, but we are a group of people who have fast internet and take video meeting bandwidth for granted. Not everyone is living that lifestyle.

Our product teams can't possibly have the full experience of the people using our software. Even if you work in "technology," company size, organizational maturity, and corporate culture can vary wildly. As soon as we start talking about software for people who do other jobs, it's unwise to assume we know what they want.

Quality user research and user persona understanding continues to be a valuable exercise. For example, as coauthor Heidi Waterhouse recalls,

I once worked for a company that was working to make the greenscreen US Medicare system more accessible and easier to use. After we had written a whole modern interface with mindfully placed buttons and dialog boxes, we gave it to the purchasing managers, who were delighted. They gave it to the back-office billing experts, who were furious.

These were people who had spent a whole career navigating the interface by function key and ten-key pad. They were blazingly fast at it and considered anything that required a mouse as an impediment to their productivity. We didn't have anyone on our team who did medical coding, and the people purchasing the system were generally younger and more "technological" than the back-office staff, so they assumed they would pick the best technology. In the end, all of us sat down and watched one of the medical coders do her work, and none of us had realized how she had been working at all. Our knowledge was flawed.

Of course, companies can't build teams that are composed of some portion of the users, but every little bit of variety in our team composition helps: someone who came from telephony, or spent some time in databases, or even, dream of dreams, people with backgrounds in library science or sociology.

Product management and marketing help us pay attention to who our customers are, who our consumers are, and who we want them to be. It also helps us ask questions like: Who are our customers in reality? How do we ensure the constraints our customers and consumers are working under align with the constraints development teams understand and build around?

If we don't build what other people want to use and buy, our business value is automatically limited to people who are just like us. That's a pretty small "total addressable market." The value of what we make is not that it's intrinsically cool; it's that it helps other people, and we can prove that it works for them.

How Do We Know What to Make?

Knowing what to build is one of the most terrifying parts of making software and one of the strongest reasons to move toward Progressive Delivery. We are making our best guess about what our consumers want, but we need to be able to respond rapidly to what they tell us and show us.

When a couple is deciding what flavor of wedding cake they want, the baker doesn't bake and decorate an entire cake for them to sample. Instead, the samples are small pieces of all the options. Software is sometimes harder to customize than cake flavors. Also, we have a business plan based on selling something to a particular demographic, and we have a vision for how to solve a business problem. We don't want to offer all possible flavors, just the ones we are willing to make into a cake.

Progressive Delivery could be seen as delivering cupcakes that can be arranged into a beautiful cake, without all the anxiety about dropping something big. We can deliver a small feature or capability and build on it as we decide what to deliver next. If all the chocolate cupcakes vanish before the vanilla, we know we should lean into chocolate. If something on the backlog supports a more elaborate chocolate delivery, maybe we should pull that into the queue next. Of course, if one of the people getting married loves lemon best, you also need to deliver that. In this analogy, the people who pay you the most are the couples getting married.

It's easy to fall into the trap of building exactly what customers ask for. It's uncomfortable to push back and ask them to describe their actual business problem, instead of the solution that they are used to. It's tempting to see a solution or implementation and try to optimize it instead of backing up and taking in the whole scenario, including the people involved, their needs, and their situation. Progressive Delivery gives us a way to start changing how we help them with a solution, without needing to have everything preplanned and implemented, so we can work together to find not just a better lamp, but a whole new world of electrification.

Progressive Delivery allows us to know what to make by helping us to more effectively:

- See how people use our products.
- Try things out before committing significant resources.
- Deliver incremental value faster.
- Get faster feedback on what we create.

OK, But...

What about things that are impossible to deliver progressively? There are people working in software environments that are not connected to any update system. We can't get progressive releases to them in a reasonable way. We can create the software using Progressive Delivery techniques, but we must deliver a fully finished, tested, and complete product. This is often life-critical software, such as for air traffic control, medical devices, or safety software.

Not every situation is right for Progressive Delivery. As champions of Progressive Delivery, we think it's a solid way of delivering value to your consumers. As experienced software people, we know there is no single solution that will fit all conditions. For Progressive Delivery to work well, you need to have all four A's: abundance, autonomy, alignment, and automation. If those aren't within your organization's reach, then Progressive Delivery is going to be difficult.

Future Proofing Ways of Working

Progressive Delivery changes some of the ways teams work in the same way that the Agile movement changed working methods for many organizations. Although many of the principles of Agile, like small batch sizes and rapid feedback, are a part of Progressive Delivery, your organization does not need to already be Agile to work toward Progressive Delivery. Here are some of the ways that Progressive Delivery future proofs your work or at least makes it more resilient in a changing environment.

Accepting and Predicting Work

Progressive Delivery emphasizes integrating customer and user feedback rapidly and continuously. Feedback is not just intentional responses but also use patterns, traffic, load, and objective and subjective metrics. Thus, when user demand around a feature or application changes, that change is incorporated in the work of the team managing it. When Progressive Delivery is working well, it tends to balance the needs of managing the system and delivering business value. Users notice features, but they also notice when they are unhappy with the performance and stability of a system they use.

That doesn't mean users drive the entire direction of a product. Rather, they are an integral part of the sensorium that affects product decisions, along with economic, technical, industry, and human factors. When we accept that our decisions are trying to solve complex socio-technical problems, we are more likely to think about solving them in more than just technical ways. We allow the scope of the problem to influence the scope of the solution we offer for it.

Design Work

How do we predict what will be needed in the future? We look to the past for the places it has been painful for us to expand. For example, if we know that we might need to localize something, we can see that taking out hard-coded language to replace it with variables is expensive and becomes more expensive the larger the interface gets. Once we've learned that lesson, we can apply it to the next project and use language variable hooks immediately, even if it's only supporting one language. There's a balance to be found between over-optimizing for the future and making everything into a problem for next year, but in general, we could stand a little more preemptive flexibility in our work.

Observing Usage

We really mean usage, in this case, and not use. Remember, you don't know how people are going to use your software, no matter what you planned. You need to see what they actually do to predict what they will want next.

- What do people use the product for?
- What problem are they solving?
- What don't they use?
- Are you forcing them to use the product the way you imagined it, or are you paving the happy path they naturally travel?

We talk about the North Star of our project and how important it is to align the team and the work to a common goal. It is important. However, Polaris, the North Star, magnetic north, and the North Pole are all actually...mutable. We can all be working toward "north" and be hundreds or thousands of miles off each other. And when it comes to company goals, these "North Stars" move all the time. It's not bad to be aligned internally as you build products, but being rigid is a great way to end up making something that doesn't meet the evolving needs of your users. A common example of this flexibility is Netflix's rise and the demise of Blockbuster.

The North Star keeps shifting. You have to focus on business value rather than implementation, and business value is tied to the value our consumers get from it. Future proofing is about actually understanding the problem we're solving, not just the tools we're using to solve it.

Building a case for change in a successful organization can be challenging. The paper "Change in a Successful Organization" categorized organizations into four "quadrants of change" to help teams identify where they were getting stuck (see Figure 10.2).[1]

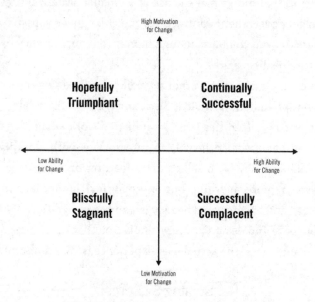

FIGURE 10.2: Quadrants of Change

Progressive Delivery exemplifies the positive aspects of creating high agility for change and providing a framework for engaging with internal and external stakeholders to create and maintain high motivation for change.

Who Are You Serving?

If you are a utility-sized company, you know it. It's a scale that very few organizations operate at. If you're not worried about antitrust lawsuits changing your workplace, then you can focus on consumers and their needs. If your business model focuses on advertisers, institutions, or other organizations that aren't your consumer, be very clear about who you are creating for. Confusion means you don't help anyone effectively. If you only have the resources to serve people who fit a certain model, be clear about that and write it down as a constraint you acknowledge. It's fine to make software that isn't localized, but don't forget that it eliminates hundreds of millions of potential users.

When your resources change, revisit your constraints. Maybe an accessibility feature that didn't make sense at a smaller scale will now make it possible to get government contracts, or multi-language support will open new markets. Maybe you have enough money to reduce latency or increase infrastructure resilience now.

For an example of products that seem like they're doing the same thing but for different audiences, look at Slack and Discord. Slack has a monthly headcount pricing, often ties your account to a work email, doesn't allow blocking, and has invested heavily in integrations with workplace tools. Discord gets its money from selling extra features on a per-user or server basis, doesn't require anything but an email for signup, lets you switch servers freely, and has invested heavily in gaming integrations. On the surface, the purpose and design are very similar, but because of the difference in intended audiences, the actual user experience is very different.

Scaling Systems

When a team creates their first rendition of a feature or product, they don't usually start by designing it to scale to millions of users. Instead, they build it small and confirm that it works. As they gain confidence in the functionality, they start to think about scaling and efficiency. How could it be more performant? How could it be more flexible for unexpected use cases? Could it be more modular so it's easy to add additional functionality and make it more useful to people? Over time, the system's architecture also has to start to account for your organizational architecture.

How do you build an organization where teams can scale at the rate they need without losing coordination and the capacity to communicate?

When a system is growing, it becomes increasingly important to identify team boundaries and dependencies. A common example is Amazon deciding that all teams needed to build their features to accept and output APIs. That allows for a crisp boundary that can be negotiated and renegotiated if it scales to an unmanageable size.

Sunsetting

Sunsetting is the act of mindfully and deliberately removing features or capabilities. For your products to grow, you have to continually sustain them and add new things. For you to not be crushed under the weight of all that, you also have to remove old and no longer useful things. You probably don't have any way to save documents to WordPro, although that was once an essential business requirement.

You know what to remove by watching use and observing what parts of your product drift into irrelevance. You know what to remove by focusing relentlessly on the problem that you're solving. Google Docs is not a spreadsheet, and Google Sheets is not a word processor; although there is a little overlap, each product is better because it's not trying to be a product that does everything at once.

Almost all features have a lifespan. There comes a time when the cost to maintain a feature is not worth what you get from it. You need to be able to mindfully remove it without disrupting the way the rest of your software works. You also want to cause a minimum disruption to anyone who is still using that feature. Ask yourself: How do we give users an alert that we're making this change? Is that effort to retain them worth what it would cost to do so?

A valuable part of sunsetting features in a Progressive Delivery world is that you can test or experiment with removing a feature without making it permanent or stressful. Removing a feature or part of a feature in a controlled way with feature flags or user settings lets you find any unknown dependencies or surprises before you remove it for all your users. It makes refactoring and incremental improvement safer and less nerve-wracking, because you can always test that everything is still working in production.

Descaling

Descaling is a specific kind of sunsetting that occurs when you reduce the resources required for your software. Once you start to sunset something or deprioritize it, how does Progressive Delivery help you scale down? You can use it to refactor and check code, and you can also use it to reduce your physical resources. Does everything still work if you change availability zones? Is there any impact on latency if you change this CDN setting? If you're wrong, you'll be able to revert it immediately.

AI: From Nice to Have to Need to Have

Generative AI has exploded into common use in the time we've been writing this book. We debated making it another "A," but as we examined that idea, we realized it's not a pillar in the same way. It's possible to add AI to any of the steps we outlined, but it's just a tool to use. The tools we use for Progressive Delivery, like incremental rollout, feature flags, cloud computing, and user telemetry, are how we're practicing Progressive Delivery, but are not the practice itself.

One significant impact AI has already had on many product development and delivery teams is that it has further increased the efficiency of code creation. This can be seen in the data from the 2024 DORA report, where 75% of respondents reported improvements in productivity.[2] However, the ability to deliver more features faster has, in some cases, exacerbated the technological jerk for many end users. This is especially true for teams and products where Progressive Delivery practices to identify an appropriate adoption cadence have not been considered.

The ability to control and maintain the consistency of interactions and workflows allows users to adopt and adapt to changes at a pace that is reasonable to them as the consumers of the product.

One of the first and most successful use cases for AI has been as a copilot technology for developers. This enabled developers and builders of products to move faster and build features more quickly. However, with this increase in speed, we do not have a way to enable people consuming products to incorporate this increased cadence more easily. Now, more than ever, we need a framework for how we can allow developers to build at a pace that is appropriate for innovation and provide a separation and control point for consumers and users to adopt at a pace that is reasonable for their abilities and use case.

As we write this, AI is still in the messy beginnings of being introduced as a new technology. In early 2025, the Gartner Hype cycle shows AI is still headed toward the peak of inflated expectations.[3] With the four A's, we have the benefit of hindsight and the ability to reflect on their actual impact.

We know AI will be a significant technology inflection point, but it is too soon to discuss it in the context of historical impact. Instead, we look at how AI is connected to each of the four A's and how those connections impact both product builders and consumers.

Abundance

AI would not be possible without abundance. The very foundation of current AI modeling, training, and rapid adoption is an abundance of compute resources. The explosion of processing units and the ability to carve up large processors (CPUs and GPUs) into smaller logical units is what lets us create large language models (LLMs) and other types of models and use those models to provide responses to queries quickly.

AI continues to consume larger and larger quantities of compute. In fact, many experts argue that to create better AI models, we are going to exceed the amount of compute and energy we can currently produce globally. This energy crisis is one of the great challenges currently facing organizations building LLMs and trying to figure out how to make them perform better without consuming as much energy.

When we spoke previously about abundance, we talked about how the compute capacity had exceeded what was needed by the applications that were currently running at the time. AI is the first workload for mass consumption that has put it to the test and has, in fact, created scarcity where before we had abundance.

In the context of Progressive Delivery, the abundance that AI brings is in the ability for generative AI to create code and other deliverables required in the build cycle that have historically been done by humans. This allows humans to leverage AI to move faster on tasks and accelerate at an even faster pace. Left unchecked, this will likely increase the technological jerk for users. But when leveraged with users in mind, this is a potentially amazing tool for building more optionality for customization or experimentation with existing resources.

Autonomy

Autonomy, like AI, has a dual implication. The first aspect of autonomy is AI itself. At its pinnacle, or final stage of advancement, AI aims to offer an autonomous computer or code that is able to think for itself and make decisions on its own. While some media outlets claim we are close to "artificial general intelligence," there is general agreement that[4] we are still likely a decade or more away from this being a reality. And some would argue that, like flying cars, we will be ten years away for many decades to come.

The other aspect of autonomy is the ability of AI to contribute to the autonomy of the individual doing the work. For different types of individual contributors who have been using AI (or in many ways simple automation) to help them with their work, we can see that there have been considerable advancements and improvements that have led to greater productivity and efficiency. Developers using AI assistance to write better code and confirm that the code they've written is actually accomplishing what they set out to do is a great example of this trend of the "AI assistant."

Another aspect of autonomy, when we start to incorporate AI, is the increase in the number of individuals who can benefit. The concept of autonomy, in the context of our reference earlier in the book, provided an opportunity for developers or builders to work on their own. In doing so, there was an implied requirement that they have a certain level of expertise or knowledge to be able to go off and work on their own projects. With AI, suddenly the bar for autonomy gets that much lower. Individuals who have no prior experience or even understanding of the steps needed to complete a goal are suddenly enabled and encouraged to be able to take on large projects, knowing they can leverage the support of an AI assistant.

In this use of generative AI assistants, we see again the tight coupling of abundance and autonomy for builders. More work is being done with even less collaboration.

As a result of this lowering of the bar for autonomous work, there's both the potential upside of increased productivity and the potential downside of exacerbating the challenge around increasing the number of work streams while decreasing focus and alignment. In addition, we run the risk that the quality of the work output may not be up to the expected standards. AI right now (in the first half of 2025) is good at helping with known unknowns: problems where there is an existing solution, but you don't know what it is. However, AI is currently not very helpful with unknown unknowns, problems where there is no preexisting solution on which the LLM has been trained. Over time, it is likely that this particular challenge can be overcome, but that starts to look more like artificial general intelligence.

Alignment

An intriguing possibility when incorporating AI is creating a system that coordinates and tracks all of the autonomous work, leveraging AI to create better alignment overall. Imagine if an AI coordination system could look at all of the independent work streams and autonomous work and help developers reconcile integration issues, reduce duplication of work, and assist with adherence to coding style and standards.

The better the AI systems become, the closer we can get to having AI understand the outcomes we are working toward, and the closer AI comes to being a better assistant in helping us get there. Of course, we run the risk that AI will look to overcorrect/overfit what we have articulated as the goal, and we will miss signals that would have recommended course correction and adjustment of the desired goal. By applying too much computer automation or AI, we run the risk of missing serendipitous or unexpected happy accidents that often result from human error and troubleshooting.

Another important aspect of alignment is when we think about how we decide on our goals or desired outcomes to begin with. This is an area where AI can, and likely will, play a role in helping us understand, aggregate, and consolidate both human feedback and feedback from the systems we're building. This can have significant benefits when we think about one of the core tenets of Progressive Delivery, which is controlling the cadence or the pace of our releases (new features or updates) to our customers and users.

AI can provide us with some insights as to how people are adopting new changes or updates when we look at the patterns of those updates over time. This can help us actually think about the cadence that would be appropriate for customers meeting certain criteria. By providing better tooling and messaging, we're setting our consumers up to be more successful with our products and services.

Alignment must not only be internal, as we work to build and deliver a product, but also external, for our customers and users. AI can help us build proxy users to test how our products are experienced by human users, without requiring actual humans. Synthetic users could be designed to have statistically possible life experiences, and an emotive AI could report on that experience.

Working with users with disabilities, we could design AIs that replicate certain kinds of cognitive or physical disabilities, which could show us how our product behaves for disabled people. This kind of synthetic data and testing is already possible, but AI and LLMs could expand on it in both volume and depth. Alignment has to start with human priorities, but to make it broadly useful, it must be automated.

Of course, there is also the potential downside of leaning too heavily on AI to provide answers to unanswered questions. A key part of alignment in Progressive Delivery is to understand the users. As we've discussed previously, alignment is about taking the time to understand the needs of your users and not just making assumptions with a limited dataset. For this reason, it's important to recognize that the way we train LLMs today means they are very good at solving previously solved problems, and if that is all you're solving, AI may get you there. But, if you're trying to solve problems that have not been solved previously, getting AI to do it may not produce the results you want.

Automation

In many ways, AI is just an extension of automation. As we were thinking about how to include AI in the context of Progressive Delivery, we often-times referred to it as simply being automated automation. Since current AI models are mostly doing a better job of searching vast amounts of information quickly and being able to assimilate responses from that information, we really aren't at the point where the AI is creating anything new. The AI is assembling things in an automated fashion, often faster than we could do it as humans.

Similarly, the challenges that we have with automation are still present with AI. If we try to do too much too fast with AI, we see the consequences. These can look like hallucinations or simply inconvenient additions of AI into products that cause more confusion than benefit to the users.

On the flipside, when applied well, AI can provide a streamlined user experience and has the benefit of reducing the level of effort needed to create a better user experience. A positive example of this would be the use of AI in the context of searching for information, where you're asking a question, and the search engine responds with an accurate AI-based assimilated answer, providing you with a reasonable context for what you were looking for. A negative example would be adding AI to a simple prescriptive work-flow, such as requesting a ride from a car service. You may not need AI (for a specific task); this can be better handled by standard automation, which avoids the operational complexity and cost of an AI process.

Understand the Present Before You Try to Build the Future

Before you can gaze into the future, you need to have a fair idea of what your present looks like. It doesn't matter to your organization what other people are doing. What matters is what you are doing and planning. Before you get excited about adding Progressive Delivery to your impressive resume, take some time to understand what kind of software delivery life cycle you have and where you are on abundance, autonomy, alignment, and automation. Will safer deployment improve anything for your customers or teammates? Or do you have bigger problems?

Some interesting context for Progressive Delivery is that there is a distinct change in what customers expect. Customers expect more voice and a vote in their interactions with software. Rather than having five options for word processing, we now have an app store with literally hundreds of options. Customers have choices, and they are going to choose things that meet their needs. If you want to be successful as a business, you need to be much more willing to listen to customers and provide the functionality they want.

What Users Want and Expect

It's not just software, either. As software is more ubiquitous in our cars, fridges, mattresses, glucose monitors, and thermostats, users are coming to demand not just features, but interoperability. They want to be able to use their phone to warm the bed and turn on the kettle before they walk through their contactless smart door. Several large companies have tried to build ecosystems/walled gardens that make interaction within their ecosystem easy to use and difficult to leave, but that is not always what users want.

We're really struggling with graceful degradation. How many of us have a Fitbit in our drawer that technically works, but the app isn't working anymore? Or a smartphone that is fine, except the battery life is terrible, and the physical battery isn't user accessible? Or documents from college that can't be opened with modern software? As we write this, right to repair is an active discussion in US courts and worlds beyond hacker conferences. If we buy something, do we own it? If we don't own it, who does?

What Do We Owe Users?

If intellectual property for tractors seems like a long way from your future considerations about software, it isn't. In the extremely near future, your car could repossess itself by driving to the dealership, your digital lock could open your door unexpectedly, and your toaster subscription could expire.

What are your ethical lines about the software you create? You should absolutely consider abusive use cases for what you are creating. If you can't think of any way to use your product for abuse, hire a security expert to investigate deeper. Future proofing is not just about how you can expand in the future, but how you might need to respond to something truly horrible.

Every new technology we get may feel, for some, like the jerk of an elevator stopping too fast, but it also presents new ways people can push boundaries or potentially *act* like jerks. The social contract is a dream where we all share cultural norms and values. But it's obvious that we don't, so build controls into your product to make it slightly harder to misuse. Be ready to turn off features that facilitate bad behavior, either globally or selectively.

Another part of preparing for a chaotic future is being mindful about what data you collect and retain. In the ad-supported internet, we collect everything we can because it makes ad profiles extremely profitable. But now we are realizing that all of us have alarmingly accurate dossiers about us in the hands of unknown data brokers. All personal data (and not just the protected PII) is like nuclear waste. It is extremely hard to dispose of, and it has a long half-life. Once you've collected it, it's seldom straightforward to dispose of it, because it's worked into so many parts of your organization.

The future has a lot of potential to make the world a better place, but taking the time to look around the corner may help your product and features remain relevant, and ideally for use cases that do not harm or exploit others. Future proofing is one of the most interesting tasks in software.

Ethical considerations are not usually a core part of how we think about our software delivery, but maybe they can be.

How to Think Like a Futurist

Now that we have hopefully convinced you that thinking about the future is an important part of your Progressive Delivery journey, you probably want some tangible advice. Here are some questions to ask yourself about your system, the tools within it, and where you want it to go.

- What is your timeline for future proofing?
- What are the risks of this software in the future?
- What are the disaster scenarios if you keep doing exactly what you're doing? Success versus failure case.
- What does "finish" mean on this project? What is enough? How will you know when you reach the end of this feature's usefulness?
- What is the next version of this feature? What will you do next?
- What are your constraints? Where are your budget limits, distribution restrictions, and chosen market segments? What is the first thing you'll run out of? What is the most you can build with what you have, and is it more than you need?
- Are you building in technical debt? Is extensibility going to double your code costs, or is it only a small percentage? Have you considered communication with other teams? Are you using proprietary formats when you could use standards?
- Is your architecture modular? Do you have scalable resources, APIs, and clear lines of communication? If you needed to swap out a tool or dependency, could you do it without disruption?
- Are you thinking about use cases for a broad range of people? Can your product be used for abuse? Is it accessible to everyone you intend to include? Do you have regulatory constraints to consider?

- If someone uses your product in a way you don't expect, do you have a way to support that? What are the explicit and implicit contracts you are making with your users?
- Do you have a trustworthy and safe way to add or remove user experiences? Can you see the consequences for users?

Conclusion

Progressive Delivery and future proofing are two sides of the same coin—one focused on delivering value today, the other on ensuring we can continue to deliver value tomorrow. Throughout this chapter, we've explored how the principles that guide effective delivery in the present can be extended to create systems resilient enough to thrive in an uncertain future.

The four A's provide not just a framework for current delivery but a foundation for sustainable evolution. By building with optionality in mind, delegating control to those closest to emerging needs, maintaining clear alignment with core user values, and automating the predictable to free resources for the unexpected—we create organizations and systems capable of adapting to whatever comes next.

Future proofing isn't about perfectly predicting tomorrow's requirements—an impossible task in our rapidly evolving technological landscape. Rather, it's about creating the conditions for graceful adaptation, allowing us to respond to change as an opportunity rather than a crisis. It's about building flexibility into our products, our processes, and our thinking.

As we move into an uncertain future, the organizations that thrive won't be those that guessed correctly about specific technologies or trends. They'll be the ones that build adaptable systems capable of evolving alongside user needs—delivering the right thing to the right person at the right time, even as all three of those elements continue to change. This is the true promise of Progressive Delivery: not just better delivery today, but sustainable delivery for all the tomorrows yet to come.

Chapter 11
CASE STUDY: DISNEY

The Walt Disney Company, or simply Disney, is one of the most recognizable brands on earth. With over two hundred thousand employees worldwide responsible for products and services as diverse as entertainment apps and streaming services to physical theme parks and cruise ships, Disney cares deeply about users and works to create experiences that are nothing short of magical.

In its over one-hundred-year history, Disney has seen its fair share of technological change. As a company, it started out as an animation studio, with 100% of its films drawn by hand, one frame at a time. Today, it is a leader in modern animation techniques, with computer-generated textures for fur or water based on fractal mathematics.

Disney is a technology innovator. Making contributions in both software and physical systems, Disney has created technology to further their pursuit of providing magical experiences. In the course of this pursuit, Disney has naturally gravitated toward a Progressive Delivery model due to their consistent and relentless focus on the user.

Disney Experiences is the division of The Walt Disney Company that includes theme parks, cruises, and products. As the name implies, this division owns all of the physical properties where Disney makes its magic come to life. From a customer perspective, this is an amazing opportunity to interact physically with Disney's imagination and magic. From a company perspective, this is an opportunity to build brand loyalty and understand user trends and sentiment toward specific customer interests.

Situation

In 2008, Disney executives realized that their guests' expectations were outpacing their ability to roll out new attractions. This was when they kicked off the "Next Generation Experience" (NGE) project, which ultimately became MyMagic+.[1] This project had the audacious goal of maximizing the time customers spent at the park.

Complication

The greatest challenge of incorporating more digital components into Disney Parks was the ability to future proof the digital components so they would last for the same duration as the physical infrastructure of the rides *and* not feel outdated. Overall, the MagicBand and the MyMagic+ projects needed to build for unknown unknowns.

Question

As an organization that is tasked with building physical infrastructure that will last for multiple decades, how does software in general, and Progressive Delivery specifically, factor into the design, build, and operation life cycle?

Answer

The DevOps approach that permeated Disney software development and site reliability engineering (SRE) teams started to encourage more modular thinking in the physical engineering of the experiences. The structural engineers started to think about how to build the experiences to allow for digital upgrades and maintenance.[2]

MagicBand

One key component of the Next Generation Experience project was the Disney MagicBand, originally announced on January 7, 2013. The MagicBand+ was built to provide a seamless authentication and access experience for guests of Disney theme parks. The goal of the project was to provide Disney with better data and greater visibility into how users interacted with the various properties while also providing a frictionless experience for guests to experience everything they wanted at the park.

The Disney MagicBand is a serendipitous benefit of incorporating Progressive Delivery practices of the right product to the right person at the right time. Even the early devices were packed full of sensors that the team thought "might" be useful. First, they had to design the physical wearable device before they knew what was going to be possible with the rest of the infrastructure and how the supporting software and hardware would change over time.

In the early days, the thought put into it was brilliant, when you look at the initial design. But there was a cost associated. By all public accounts, the team didn't even know what would stick. So, when considering what components and sensors to include, they didn't know what would be most useful. So, they overloaded the hardware, beginning with capabilities that would allow it to be extendable. This provided optionality for future growth and experimentation. Abundance enabled this approach due to the advances in technology that made these sensors small enough and cheap enough to be included in a wearable device in the first place.

This long-term planning was part of the consideration from the early days of the project. In the sense of future proofing, they didn't know precisely what would be most helpful to users, but they had some general ideas. Some things are obvious, like door locks. After all, it was going to be "your key to the kingdom." The MagicBand was the pass to the park and your key to your room (if you were staying in a Disney property). These choices led to some basic requirements, like an RFID chip. This was later joined by Bluetooth, LEDs, an accelerometer, and some on-device memory.

The vision was to enable wearers to make purchases, use the device for park entry, and even do some things that could be actioned based on their geography. Since the goal was to maximize engagement and make every customer's experience feel magical, personalization is a great way to make people feel special. Knowing where people are in proximity to some experience, personalized content could be shown to the wearer that would further enhance their unique experience.

Soon, the teams realized that wearables could leverage the explosion of smartphones and be used as paired devices. Later, the phone could replace the device for users if they chose. This meant the wearable could be updated and manipulated by the smartphone to offer even greater functionality without changing the experience of the person wearing the device by needing to add more sensors. In fact, in some cases, the Disney team started looking at what they could remove from the MagicBand since they could expect a paired smartphone to be present.

Suddenly, the same population that Disney initially focused on went from needing a wearable everywhere they went to actually having something that was very noisy and emitting all the signals the park needed from their pocket, a cell phone. Because of the loosely coupled approach that had been taken with the overall project, the team was able to quickly pivot and take advantage of this physical technological shift. The teams were able to autonomously work on the features associated with different sensors due to the architectural choices of loose coupling and leveraging open standards.

As more sensors were introduced in smartphones and more users began to use the Disney App, there was the ability to observe and reduce the number of sensors in the MagicBand to make room for new ones, and things like a rechargeable battery. They could progressively release new features in the App on the phone as sensors and features were added. Instead of requiring their custom hardware, the MagicBand, the functionality could live in the software and be hardware agnostic.

Of course, for many, a $35 wearable continues to be a preferred device to gain access to all the Disney magic instead of handing your five-year-old a smartphone. However, even in this case, the ability to connect to a paired smartphone can update settings and help you keep track of your kids' activities in the park.

All of this technology has enabled Disney to exceed its original goal of maximizing the time customers spend at the park and create experiences tailored to the individual.

Beyond the Band

The MagicBand is an early example of Disney's forward-looking approach to digital technologies. In more recent years, this has expanded to the rides themselves, which have increasingly embraced technology and become examples of leading-edge cyber-physical systems. The lessons learned about the power of software, coupled with thoughtful hardware choices, continue to make the MagicBand a magical experience.

From Liability to Asset

Initially, digital components were one of the most burdensome aspects of physical attractions. The physical steel, concrete, plastics, and paint were easier to stress test, they had predictable replacement timelines, and replacement parts could be manufactured across decades to the same specifications (even from third-party suppliers). This was not always the case for digital components, because the technology changed so quickly.

There are elements of safety-critical components in the system. Even the software controls the speed or literal jerk of large mechanical motors as part of these attractions. You need some way to evaluate and test changes and new code that you're building. It is not economical to build a full mockup of the attraction. Instead, Disney creates some simulators[3]—digital twins—of the physical attraction that can be used as a prototype. This becomes a stage in the Progressive Delivery of updates to the digital experiences. New code gets built and deployed to the digital twin for validation. Then, the code can be safely deployed to the physical experience.

Disney's newer environments even have the ability to do isolated rollouts to allow for non-destructive testing with explicitly targeted audiences.

Maintenance used to be about painting or re-landscaping at the attraction. Now they need to factor in things like software updates and upgrades. With this, there needs to be some consideration of the modern-day equivalent of re-mulching and pruning trees. What is the corollary of software landscaping? What do you do for the software experience that has all these interactivities that the guests are either bringing with them or participating in? Now, the system itself observes through vision systems, and they are able to track you and follow your motions. This is how they deliver an immersive, unique, magical experience. But how do you take that to the next level? And what do you plan for, knowing that in five years, people want something new? Twenty years for a teacup ride has one set of maintenance expectations; twenty years for an interactive experience looks very different.

Deployment vs. Release in Physical Systems

When you're working on physical systems, especially at the scale of an attraction at a Disney property, the idea of a progressive release looks a little different. Disney is thinking about that early on and baking it into their software delivery pipelines. How they develop the ability to get feedback loops at all the different stages in a very practical way allows them to get to a place where they can even test in production. Even in the physical attraction. Developers can see the new code while sitting inside a ride. They can make the change, commit it—using their approved peer review process—and see the changes show up on the next cycle through the ride.

This type of testing in production is done in a downtime maintenance state or renovation state, which is coupled with other physical upgrades that may occur, but the power testing of the changes in the production system at this pace is impressive. Because now they've brought those feedback loops to the edge, where their production environment really is. Disney Imagineers are able to see it and make creative changes in near real time.

This is how Disney can test in production with practically zero impact on customers.

Making Staging Look Like Production

Another challenge of digital-physical systems is the ability to make your staging environment match your production environment. Software manages controller logic for show systems and for ride vehicle systems. Disney had to figure out how to update that continuously. It had to be automatable and deployable. This changed the way they had to think about their deployment pipeline. Suddenly, they had to think about it in multiple contexts and multiple environments. When they are deploying, is it to a digital twin or into the physical production system? They need to keep both of those in sync as much as possible. This is needed to avoid doing work twice and having to train on two different systems.

As Jason Cox said in his presentation at the DevOps Enterprise Summit Amsterdam in 2023,

> We ship happiness, [but] how about bringing happiness to those who are creating. Faster release cycles, creating self-service, low-friction ways for them to be able to deliver, handing back time to our engineers, handing back time and empowering our artists to create these new experiences, these new characters, these new worlds that delight our guests. And ultimately amplifying our creativity across the company.[4]

As an example, Cox shared his team's experience working on the Millennium Falcon ride, commonly known as Smugglers Run. "We helped the Imagineers build CI/CD. So, it delivers all the way out to the edge. You could sit in the ride vehicle, see a problem, open up your laptop, check out the code, fix what you wanted, change it right there in the ride vehicle, check it back in, and on the next cycle you would see your code in production."[5]

This allowed the team to see problems, experiment, and perfect. Cox explained,

Drive quality, right? We've done that over and over again. [We] did that again with web slingers. We've done that with our Galactic Starcruiser. And what we heard...from our parks [business] was, "That was the smoothest, easiest launch of any attraction we've ever seen."...It wasn't like we were using a new technology. No, we allowed them to see problems and then addressed them in a faster [low-friction] way.[6]

As Cox added,

We've done the same thing with attractions handing back Imagineers the opportunity to sit on a ride vehicle, see a problem, a defect, and check out the code. [They can] pull open their laptop, edit, upload, see it build, and on very next cycle see their code in the attraction in production. What does that allow for greater iteration to polish improve quality. Experiment. Deliver more magical experiences for our guests. We sent that into orbit and back on Earth we're reminded we got to actually help. Build community build trust and build magic together.[7]

A Progressive Delivery approach to progressive releases and isolation of the impact radius to just the development team has provided tremendous value. Teams can deploy new versions of software to the attractions with far less effort, and in some newer attractions, provide different experiences to different visitors based on identifying users through their smartphone or MagicBand. This personalized approach further increases the core metric of in-park engagement.

Summary

Disney is an interesting example of Progressive Delivery in a combined digital-physical environment. Disney leveraged abundance, such as reduced component costs, to allow Imagineers to build infrastructure that was expandable and enhanced through software over time.

Embracing autonomy encouraged the use of software to increase value over time and leveraged open standards to provide flexibility in the hardware that was required to have the best possible experience. As an organization, alignment at Disney meant the software teams could understand the constraints of the systems they were working on. This led to the creation of digital twins to better test and experiment with the physical structures. This also had the benefit of empowering the Imagineers responsible for the physical designs to make updates to provide more accessible structures for the teams responsible for updating the digital components over the lifespan of the experience.

Automation has been implemented in the software development pipeline and has also helped to create more predictable outcomes for maintenance and upgrades. All of these things have combined to create a Progressive Delivery experience that leads to greater user engagement and more sustainable and cost-beneficial physical infrastructure.

Chapter 12

OUROBOROS

You are not obligated to complete the task, but neither are you free to desist from it.

—**Pirke Avot** 2:21

This isn't the first time people have faced the jerk of technology. We're not saying it hasn't happened before. Rather, we're saying the rate of change is speeding up.

In the past century, we've seen how massive transformations have changed the world around us and continue to do so at an ever-increasing rate. It's not so much the change that has become uncomfortable, but the rate at which change continues to push through nearly every aspect of our lives.

When companies are facing a transformational change, they don't have to collapse, nor do they need to change everything. With Progressive Delivery, an organization can change iteratively and strategically instead of a destabilizing force. The jerk can be a positive change agent.

A jerk can throw you off balance. When the train lurches or the elevator drops from under you, you're untethered. It can feel like you're in free fall. But you have the ability to change direction, to pivot, and make a decision on where you'd like to go next. You have it all, but you need to be honest about where you are and what you're working with. What is your abundance? How much autonomy does your team have? How aligned are you? Are you automating where possible? If you try to maintain what you had before, you will fall. Or at best, you will try to cling to that which was. Be Netflix, not Blockbuster.

Jerk as a Change Agent

Though we've focused on how the rate of change has increased dramatically in recent years, even this feeling of jerk is not new. The arrival of the internet in the 1990s was an incredible jerk for the retail industry. It changed so much of our understanding of what the consumer relationship is to stores and how people connect with them.

It's hard to imagine a time before online shopping existed. Today, you can purchase nearly anything—from books to clothes, fresh groceries, furniture, or even a car—and have it delivered within a matter of hours. Most brands have some kind of online presence. If they don't have their own website where they sell their products, they likely connect to a third-party site that enables them to do so. People of all backgrounds casually purchase goods and services online, often from the convenience of their smartphones whenever inspiration strikes.

However, some of us may recall the early days of online shopping back in the twentieth century. If you were lucky enough to have access to a computer that could get online, you could buy books on Amazon.com, bid for items on eBay, or order from Pizza Hut's PizzaNet portal.[1] In those halcyon days of Web 2.0, websites were flat and simple, loading could take many minutes, and this usually occurred from a large, heavy computer that sat on a table with a fan furiously buzzing inside of it.

Waiting minutes for a page to load is excruciating by today's standards, but in that moment, it was incredible. The internet was a new experience that many wanted a glimpse of. People could connect with each other in ways unheard of before. They could talk to friends, family, or colleagues hundreds of miles away. They could access large volumes of information from the comfort of that desktop computer. And they could shop for things without having to travel to an actual store. From the years 1995 to 2000, the number of internet users grew from 44.8 million to over 413 million, and the number of websites jumped from 23,500 to over 17 million.[2]

Some companies failed to catch the wave and slowly faded out, whereas others caught the wave and rode it into a new era. One company that not only caught a wave but redefined the consumer experience in a way that still reverberates throughout the retail industry today is Nike.

A Moment of Transformation at Nike

By 1998, Nike was one of the leading athletic apparel brands in the world with an over $11 billion market cap.[3] Their infamous swoosh and eponymous tagline were recognized by people of all ages around the world. Their shoes and clothing were loved within athletic circles and pop culture alike. Basketball fans lined up annually for the latest Air Jordans. Nike was featured prominently within the internationally beloved Soccer World Cup, and rap artist Jay-Z had fans clamoring for Air Force 1s.

Like every other major consumer brand, they knew the internet was where they needed to be. However, a creative team within the organization wanted to do more than just show up on the internet with another static website. To them, the internet represented an opportunity to deliver an experience. It was the first time there was a technology in place that could reach people wherever they were. They saw this as a new communications channel that was an exciting new means to an end.

"Before NIKEiD, only our shoe designers could design shoes. So, in some sense, NIKEiD was an expression of pushing capabilities that only shoe designers had to the customer. It's an obvious statement, but I want to ground ourselves there. This was the genesis of NIKEiD," said Ron Forrester.[4]

The concept centered around the customer. It offered customers a connection to the brand, it provided access in a way unrealized before, and it celebrated loyal fans. Nike had already proven itself a global powerhouse with a large and consistent fan base. This experience, if delivered well, could further strengthen that bond.

The Challenges of Being the First

It's important to remember that the NIKEiD concept came from a creative team on the business side of Nike, not engineering. "I think if anything drove us toward something different, it was the fact that the engineering capabilities were seen as something that was stopping the business from growing at the rate that it wanted to grow," said Forrester.

That isn't to say that engineering wasn't doing enough. Rather, Nike was willing to provide support for any area that needed investment so that new ideas could be realized. There was a culture of innovation within the organization that promised copious resources whenever necessary. Nike was prepared to do whatever was necessary so they could move at the speed of the consumer.

In this moment, building an interactive site for the internet was a priority. On the consumer-facing side, it had to be ready to sustain large traffic loads, and it needed to support a range of high-quality images that showcased the product. Ultimately, they wanted to ensure the experience would inspire customers to actually pay for the product. On the business-facing side, the site needed to integrate with the existing systems for production. This included Nike's corporate headquarters as well as their factories where the actual shoes were to be constructed.

"As technologists, our response was elasticity, autonomy, abundance, infrastructure, not having to wait three months to get a new server and all those things," explained Forrester.

Engineers also had to consider autonomy, alignment, and automation when delivering this product. Engineering fully recognized how important it was to provide business teams with access to the platform on a deeper level, delegating power to product managers so that decisions could be made in concert with the business.

Furthermore, their system needed to align with manufacturing. This not only needs to meet customer expectations but also to streamline production. Specific shoe designs and materials available were carefully controlled, and there was an opportunity to use this system to provide visibility necessary for teams to align around.

Though Nike was a large global entity at this point, they needed to proceed carefully with how they rolled out this experience. They wanted to be sure that manufacturing could scale to meet demand without compromising quality or exceeding budgets.

Abundance Made Me Do It

The foundation for the NIKEiD project was built on racked servers. Though they were finite and could only do so much, the organization made sure to provide the maximum the team could ever need. For the Nike team, this meant designing and implementing infrastructure that can handle the traffic of a new shoe launch. Even when that new shoe is associated with a famous Los Angeles Laker, and Nike drops the custom design on the day of his last game.

Then the engineers had to consider how to visualize the product. "The hard part about customization is figuring out how to visualize the thing for the consumer so they're willing to give you money for it," said Sam Gordon.[5]

Initially, this aspect of the experience was rooted in photography. Emphasis was placed on taking quality images of the shoes as finished products. Afterward, the photos were sliced into gray-scale images using photo tools. The user experience on the web would essentially rebuild a shoe using the sliced-up image segments, applying the consumer's desired color and pattern choices to each segment on demand.

It was essential that this image compositing was performed as quickly as possible to help the consumer envision their choices in real time. Careful attention was paid to color and hex code matching to ensure that what was displayed on the web would match the real product as closely as possible. Remember, this is happening around 1998 to 1999, when a 100MB image was considered large.

As the project proved successful, Nike allowed it to evolve. Different shoe models and material combinations were rolled out. And, of course, as their system evolved, their practices grew with it. When cloud-native and open-source technologies became available, the team found ways to incorporate them into their system. They moved from managed datacenters, racking and stacking, to a cloud-native strategy. Instead of waiting months to push updates or add new features, they now ship code daily.

This photography-based, cloud-hosted solution served Nike well for many years, but eventually, product designers were constrained by what the user experience could visualize for consumers. The web experience was unable to successfully visualize an iridescent material, for instance, so the consumer could see color and light change as the shoe was seen at different angles. The use of different materials with texture was difficult in the photography-based solution.

3D designers were brought in to model products with realistic replications of shoes that replaced the need for photography. The engineering team needed to advance their application by introducing a 3D rendering platform to unlock the ideas of shoe designers. Color and pattern options were bolstered by texture and material options to overlay on 3D models for an even more realistic virtual rendering of a product.

New challenges became unlocking questions such as: Can you see how a suede will appear differently than a kidskin leather? How will this material appear when stretched over this particular curve of the shoe?

"It was not dissimilar from building, you know, a website that people touch and feel," said Gordon.

The move to cloud-native technology, combined with the advent of 3D modeling, unlocked the engineering team's ability to solve this new challenge. Scale of infrastructure was no longer a concern. Access to new types of infrastructure, such as GPU-based on-demand servers, unlocked the 3D visualization piece of the puzzle.

What was interesting about the 3D platform they built was that it served all of their constituents. It was helpful for business teams in terms of planning and strategy. Lead times were shortened by being able to visualize finished products in 3D without requiring the need for physical samples to be manufactured. They could experiment with different models and materials before making them available to the public.

It was refined and compelling for consumers. It enabled the average person to design a shoe like a professional designer, even showing a realistic representation of what different color and material combinations could provide.

This system was also incredibly helpful for manufacturing when it came time to actually build these custom pieces. It not only connected to existing infrastructure within the factory, allowing the pieces for each custom shoe to be collected more efficiently, but workers could more easily visually QA their work.

Progressive Delivery as an Ongoing Practice

In the twenty-five years since NIKEiD was first launched, the ability to build customized consumer goods has exploded. Consumers can design a range of products from cars (BMW and Ferrari) to cookies (Oreos). There are now engines that you can plug into your Shopify storefront to do many of the same things that Nike had to figure out from first principles.

NIKEiD now generates a "significant revenue and a large portion of our total e-commerce business," said Ken Dice, Nike's vice president of NIKEiD.[6]

The lesson we should take from Nike is not that they make custom shoes, but that the entire company contributed resources and abundance to follow through on the creative team's vision. It's tempting to parcel out resources to each team in proportion to how much they bring in, but sometimes, a burst of abundance in a focused area levels up the capacities of the whole company.

The most constraining factor in the environment was the early web's capacity to serve variable images, coupled with retooling the factories to perform customization. Nike prioritized delivering a high-quality experience and initially was willing to invest in providing whatever hardware resources were necessary to host the site. Abundance.

Nike provided their engineers the resources and autonomy necessary to build and maintain a system that could deliver the graphics necessary. This was in keeping with their tight alignment around brand standards. If they were going to provide an experience, it had to be of a certain quality. It was understood that if there weren't a tool available, then they'd build it. For good measure, these high-quality graphics were useful for internal business and manufacturing partners, providing these teams with the autonomy they needed while still keeping everyone aligned.

It's also worth noting that alignment included a range of constituents. This effort included groups across Nike—product, engineering, marketing, manufacturing, and their customers. It started with the product team; they had a strong vision born out of real feedback from their customers. It relied on engineers to bring this concept to reality. The experience was delivered in such a way that the product, manufacturing, and the Nike customer could remain grounded together. Not only was this helpful for maintaining alignment, but it also enabled Nike to scale its efforts efficiently in the future.

Although NIKEiD was a big bet for Nike, it was a bet, and not the core of their business, which continued to focus on in-person sales and retail partners. The size of their bet was dictated by the health of the rest of the business. Over time, the bet has paid off.

While Nike might not look back on this story with the language of Progressive Delivery, it includes the core tenets we've outlined in this book: abundance, autonomy, alignment, and automation. In the case of Nike, the technological jerk of innovation propelled them ahead of their competition and directly aligned them with building the right thing for the right people at the right time.

Recap and Takeaways

As we've repeated from the beginning, Progressive Delivery is about delivering the right thing to the right people at the right time, in the interest of all the constituents.

We have interviewed people doing that, added our own combined century of experience, and suggested patterns and processes—but we can only give you the outline of how it will work for you and your organization. Look at what you have in abundance and imagine using it better. Give people the autonomy to choose their own most important features, both on your team and for your users. Communicate about what the goal is and how you think you can align to get there together. Make the simple things automatic and the hard things as simple as possible with automation.

Remember, no single set of people gets to say what something is—it is what they are experiencing and making. What each person brings to the software that shapes experience is as important as the intentions of the people making it.

Progressive Delivery is an invitation to look at what you already have and use it better. This book was structured to show you different parts of a Progressive Delivery system, both in the abstract, with our A's chapters, and in the concrete, with the case studies.

- We laid out some patterns and ways of building software to get you started thinking about what Progressive Delivery looks like.
- We wrote about abundance and how having more than the bare minimum of resources necessary makes it possible to do exciting and creative things.
- We talked about how autonomy is important to both the people creating something and the people consuming it, because we don't all want the same things at the same time, and we aren't all made happy by the same things.
- We discussed alignment and how vital it is on both the internal and external levels. Working with a group to make something is great. Working to make something that people find useful and meaningful is amazing.
- We wrote about automation and how useful it is to make everything that can possibly be left to a machine, up to machines, so humans can get on with doing interesting, creative, or caring work.
- We told you about future proofing, and how to consider your plans and investments for the next steps.

Each case study contained elements of all of our pillars, but we highlighted the ones that were particularly relevant to the preceding chapter.

This book is just one part of the conversation about Progressive Delivery. Keep your eyes out for other examples of how delivering incrementally, responding to changing needs, cultivating autonomy and alignment, and putting effort toward what matters to users show up in all sorts of places.

You Already Live in a Progressive Delivery World

Progressive Delivery is not zero-sum; it's generative. Even if you don't have much abundance, you can start using automation to free up resources. Even if the full magical feedback from users is unavailable, you can still take small steps toward aligning with them and their needs, which will give you a little more slack for abundance. Anywhere you can improve one A, you gain a little more room to work on the rest, and your system gets a bit better.

We started writing about Progressive Delivery in the context of software, because that's where we were focusing, but as we've been researching this book, we have seen it in so many places. We've been sending each other examples as we wrote—mRNA vaccines, knit-along patterns, college syllabi, automotive behavior, and KitKat flavors. We can't stop seeing it. Removing dams on the Klamath River so salmon can once again migrate? It took the abundance of solar power to make hydroelectricity less important, and it took alignment with the tribal stakeholders to push for the actual removal. Using cars as satellite hotspots in a disaster zone? That takes autonomy to turn the capability on quickly and automation to target and deliver it correctly.

We can't tell you that adopting a certain set of practices is going to fix your culture or that you can bootstrap your way into being a generative Progressive Delivery organization. We're also not here to tell you what you shouldn't do. We don't know your constraints and limitations.

We do hope that this book has given you a "critical lens" shaped like Progressive Delivery so that you can have the same awareness of possible options and modes for your organization. What we're describing is not novel, you just may not have had a name for it. With this critical lens, you'll be able to look at many of the situations in your life and ask yourself: "Could there be more abundance? Could there be more automation?"

If the problem is toddlers fighting over who gets the blue plate, get more blue plates and allow them to have what they want and express their autonomy. If the problem is remembering to take your pills every day, putting them in a pill keeper is a kind of automation, and it allows you to meet your long-term goals for your health (alignment).

This only forms a virtuous cycle if we remember "in the interest of all the constituents." We originally thought that fast fashion was an example of Progressive Delivery, but it exploits everyone who makes the clothes and ignores both the upstream and downstream effects on the environment. It is superficially aligned with consumers and grants them autonomy and abundance, but it is not generative if it hurts humans and our ecosystem.

You'll know if you're looking at a Progressive Delivery system if an increase in any of the A's makes it easier to increase the others and if we consider constituents beyond just the customer, including the creators, patients, system integrators, repair techs, and biomes that the system affects.

Future Shock Absorber and Inertial Dampener

We can make machines that go unfathomably fast. What we can't do yet is make machines that go unfathomably fast without killing us: the squishy meat parts of any technical system. Bullet trains can't just start up at full speed; they need to accelerate and decelerate smoothly to prevent passenger injury.

Humans have finite tolerances for the rate of change that our bodies can handle. We also have finite, but variable, tolerances for the rate of change we can accept in how our world works. When we talk about stressful life changes, the stress comes from the amount of change, not necessarily whether we think the change is positive.

Organizations also have a finite rate of change and stress tolerances. They are not always the same across parts of the organization, nor are they linear, but they are real. A smooth acceleration is easier to handle than a sudden change or pivot, but planning a smooth acceleration is a hard problem that often entails stops and starts and sudden jerks.

As Alvin Toffler wrote in *Future Shock* in 1970, the impact of jerk (the acceleration of acceleration) can be significant:

> *The acceleration of change in our time is, itself, an elemental force. This accel-*
> *erative thrust has personal and psychological, as well as sociological, con-*
> *sequences. ...unless man quickly learns to control the rate of change in his*
> *personal affairs as well as in society at large, we are doomed to a massive*
> *adaptational breakdown.*[7]

In the fifty years since Toffler predicted the impact of accelerated change, much of what he predicted has come to pass.

On the positive side, we have found ways to use technology to accommodate rapid change. From the lowest levels where we have implemented error correction in the components of silicon to the macro level where we can make accurate forecasts of our environment, we use technology. On the negative side, our existence is mediated by enormous stacks of technology we neither understand nor control.

When Toffler was writing in 1970, rural electrification and telephone service were still working their way to unwired parts of the United States, and they were very much part of his living memory. Now we have a few isolated places beyond common cell phone reach. Our emergencies do not require running to the nearest house with a telephone, but when a cascading outage takes our 911 call centers offline. When it's freezing cold and the power goes out, it is no longer possible for most people to heat their homes themselves by burning something.

The shocks Toffler foresaw fifty years ago are both prescient and funny from our vantage point. He was remarkably right about changes in education, and in some of his predictions about family structure, about how dislocation and disconnection would affect us culturally and emotionally. He foresaw telecommunications, but not the portability or power. We aren't all living in undersea communes, and a lot of his futuring-in-communities sounds like excruciating committee meetings. However, it's useful to understand the core of his argument—that change is not only an individual adaptation problem, but a collective challenge.

Reading a long-ago futurist makes us cautious about our own predictions. We know that change is a constant part of our world, and nothing
indicates that it will slow down. In fact, we can probably expect at least one
or two more "jerks" in our careers, where the paradigm changes enough
that it causes a crisis of training and leadership. This book is intended to
describe the lurch that you are feeling now or beginning to feel—the movement from software as something bestowed on users to a conversation with
users.

The core of Progressive Delivery is that we can look at abundance,
autonomy, alignment, and automation and use them to deliver the right
experience to users as they need it. Disney is building physical infrastructure that has to be both durable and responsive to changing guest needs.
Nike is delivering *au courant* customized consumer goods.

Both organizations benefit from planning their organization to
respond flexibly to inputs and their structure to build and deliver nuanced
and individual experiences. Adobe is mindfully testing both the experience
of using their software and the experience of creating it, in ways intended
to deliver the right thing. GitHub continues to leverage Progressive
Delivery to provide a delightful user experience to the ever-increasing community of global developers.

The concept that brings the ideas of adapting to rate of change, our
four A's, and future proofing together in the single concept we are calling
"Progressive Delivery" is adaptation. As each part of our organizations and
world changes, we must adapt to it. Even heritage businesses with hundreds of years of making the same thing now have web sites and social
media accounts, because that's how they will survive until the next change,
and the next.

Leon Megginson, a professor of management and marketing, para-
phrased Darwin thus:

> According to Darwin's Origin of Species, *it is not the most intellectual of the
> species that survives; it is not the strongest that survives; but the species that
> survives is the one that is able best to adapt and adjust to the changing envi-
> ronment in which it finds itself.*[8]

"Survival of the fittest" is not, as we sometimes misunderstand it, about strength. It's about fitness, about being the right thing for the environment and ecosystem you currently exist in.

Call to Action:
What Are We Going to Do About All This?

We hope that our descriptions and examples in this book have helped you see the characteristics of Progressive Delivery and think about where you may already be practicing them or where you could explore further. Trying to change your whole speed of delivery or operation may be too great a rate of change, but you can accelerate parts here and there to start seeing valuable changes. One of the first things that we recommend is identifying all your constituents and seeing if it's possible to align more closely with them.

We've told you a lot about what Progressive Delivery is. Let us tell you what it's not. It's not zero-sum. It's not about winners and losers. Progressive Delivery is not a competition. It's about using all the tools we have to build something nourishing for ourselves, our organizations, and our world.

If the buses come more often, more people will be able to ride them. It's not that we don't have enough riders for an hour; it's that we only have so many riders that wait an hour. And the reason we have zero-sum thinking is because we are limited by a lack of abundance, autonomy, alignment, and automation.

There's a children's story that many of us read called *Stone Soup*. In the story, a stranger comes to a hungry town and starts a fire under a cauldron of water. He puts a magic stone in to make stone soup. As the villagers watch him, he talks about how much he's looking forward to his stone soup, but, ah, it would be even better with a little bit of onion. One by one, the villagers contribute the small scraps of food that they can, until there is a rich soup enough to feed everyone.

Progressive Delivery is a kind of stone soup. We have provided the pot, and the water, and the stone to shape the magic. We know, from our decades of experience, that you have the cabbage or a Parmesan rind that you can throw in the pot. Start there.

BIBLIOGRAPHY

Atlassian. "State of the Developer Report." 2022. https://atlassianblog.wpengine.com/wp-content/uploads/2022/03/atlassian-state-of-the-developer-report-pdf.pdf.

Bazen, Alexus. "Cell Phone Statistics 2025." ConsumerAffairs, December 2, 2024. https://www.consumeraffairs.com/cell_phones/cell-phone-statistics.html.

Beck, Kent, Mike Beedle, Arie van Bennekum, Alistair Cockburn, Ward Cunningham, Martin Fowler, James Grenning, et al. "Manifesto for Agile Software Development." 2001. Accessed February 25, 2025. https://agilemanifesto.org/.

C, Ben. "How Disney Uses Digital Twins to Maintain Its Most Innovative Rides," Radix, October 15, 2024. https://radix-communications.com/how-disney-uses-digital-twins-to-maintain-its-most-innovative-rides/.

Chacon, Scott. "Scott Chacon on the Interwebs." August 31, 2011. https://web.archive.org/web/20111112170214/http://scottchacon.com/2011/08/31/github-flow.html.

Cox, Jason. "Disney Global SRE – Creating Digital Magic," presented at DevOps Enterprise Summit, Las Vegas, 2022. https://videos.itrevolution.com/watch/762364309?start=1131.

Cox, Jason. "Disney Global SRE – Creating Digital Magic," presented at DevOps Enterprise Summit, Amsterdam, 2023. https://videos.itrevolution.com/watch/830906711?start=1246.

Department of the Navy. "The Commanding Officer." Accessed February 26, 2025. https://www.secnav.navy.mil/doni/US%20Navy%20Regulations/Chapter%208%20-%20The%20Commanding%20Officer.pdf.

DORA. "Accelerate: State of DevOps 2018: Strategies for a New Economy." 2018. https://services.google.com/fh/files/misc/state-of-devops-2018.pdf.

DORA. "Accelerate: State of DevOps 2024." 2024. https://dora.dev/research/2024/dora-report/.

Edmondson, Amy. *The Fearless Organization: Creating Psychological Safety in the Workplace for Learning, Innovation, and Growth.* John Wiley & Sons, 2013.

Evans, Julia. "What Happens When You Press a Key in Your Terminal?" July 20, 2022. https://jvns.ca/blog/2022/07/20/pseudoterminals/.

FinOps Foundation. "What Is FinOps?" Accessed February 25, 2025. https://www.finops.org/introduction/what-is-finops/.

Gartner. "Gartner Hype Cycle Research Methodology." Accessed February 25, 2025. https://www.gartner.com/en/research/methodologies/gartner-hype-cycle.

GitLab. "Blue-Green Deployment ($1846041) · Snippets · GitLab." Accessed February 25, 2025. https://gitlab.com/-/snippets/1846041.

Henshall, W. "When Might AI Outsmart Us? It Depends Who You Ask." Time, January 19, 2024. https://time.com/6556168/when-ai-outsmart-humans/.

Hicks, Catherine M. "Psychological Affordances Can Provide a Missing Explanatory Layer for Why Interventions to Improve Developer Experience Take Hold or Fail." PsyArXiv, January 25, 2024. doi:10.31234/osf.io/qz43x.

Humble, Jez, and David Farley. Continuous Delivery: Reliable Software Releases Through Build, Test, and Deployment Automation. Boston: Pearson, 2010.

IT Revolution. "Change in a Successful Organization." August 14, 2024. https://itrevolution.com/product/change-in-a-successful-organization/.

IT Revolution. "Leadership Development and Balancing Creativity and Control With Admiral John Richardson." November 28, 2023. https://www.youtube.com/watch?v=IWOnTAPSZko.

Knight Capital Americas LLC. "Order Instituting Administrative And Cease-And-Desist Proceedings, Pursuant To Sections 15(B) And 21c Of The Securities Exchange Act Of 1934, Making Findings, And Imposing Remedial Sanctions And A Cease-And-Desist Order." Report. Securities And Exchange Commission, October 16, 2013. https://www.sec.gov/files/litigation/admin/2013/34-70694.pdf.

Kuang, Cliff. "Disney's $1 Billion Bet on a Magical Wristband." WIRED, March 10, 2015. https://www.wired.com/2015/03/disney-magicband/.

Liker, Jeffrey. The Toyota Way: 14 Management Principles from the World's Greatest Manufacturer. New York: McGraw Hill, 2004.

The Lego Movie. Directed by Phil Lord and Christopher Miller. Warner Bros. and Village Roadshow, 2014.

Lovelace, Ada. Ada, the Enchantress of Numbers. Mill Valley, CA: Strawberry Press, 1992. https://openlibrary.org/books/OL1571641M/Ada_the_enchantress_of_numbers.

Lufkin, Bryan. "The Curious Origins of Online Shopping." February 25, 2022. https://www.bbc.com/worklife/article/20200722-the-curious-origins-of-online-shopping.

Majors, Charity. "So You Want to Build an Observability Tool..." Honeycomb, August 26, 2024. https://www.honeycomb.io/blog/so-you-want-to-build-an-observability-tool.

Marquet, L. David. Turn the Ship Around!: A True Story of Turning Followers into Leaders. New York: Portfolio, 2013.

Maslach, Christina, and Susan E. Jackson. "The Measurement of Experienced Burnout." Journal of Organizational Behavior 2, no. 2 (April 1, 1981): 99–113. https://doi.org/10.1002/job.4030020205.

McLeod, Sal. "Harry Harlow Monkey Experiments: Cloth Mother Vs Wire Mother," *Simply Psychology*. June 15, 2023. https://www.simplypsychology.org/harlow -monkey.html.

Megginson, Leon C. "Lessons From Europe for American Business," *The Southwestern Social Science Quarterly* 44, no. 1 (1963): 3–13. https://www.jstor.org/stable/ 42866937.

Mills, Kim, and Christina Maslach. "Why We're Burned Out and What to Do About It, With Christina Maslach, PhD." Speaking of Psychology podcast, episode 152. American Psychological Association, July 2021. https://www.apa.org/news/pod-casts/speaking-of-psychology/burnout.

Moore, Geoffrey. *Crossing the Chasm: Marketing and Selling Disruptive Products to Mainstream Customers*. New York: Harper Collins, 1991.

Moore, Gordon E. "Cramming More Components Onto Integrated Circuits." Electronics, April 1965, 114–17. https://www.cs.utexas.edu/~fussell/courses/cs352h/ papers/moore.pdf.

"Nike (NKE) - Market Capitalization." Accessed March 17, 2025. https://companies-marketcap.com/nike/marketcap/.

"NikeID: Polishing the Shoe Buying Experience." Technology and Operations Management, November 17, 2016. https://d3.harvard.edu/platform-rctom/submission/ nikeid-polishing-the-shoe-buying-experience/.

OpenLibrary.org. "Ada, the Enchantress of Numbers by Ada Lovelace | Open Library." 1992. https://openlibrary.org/books/OL1571641M/Ada_the_enchantress_of_ numbers.

Parkinson, C. Northcote. *Parkinson's Law, or the Pursuit of Progress*. London: Penguin, 1958.

Pink, Dan. *Drive: The Surprising Truth About What Motivates Us*. New York: Riverhead Books, 2011.

Puppet Labs, IT Revolution Press, and ThoughtWorks. "2014 State of DevOps Report." 2014. https://dora.dev/research/2014/2014-state-of-devops-report.pdf.

Reuters. "Sonos CEO Patrick Spence Steps Down After App Update Debacle." January 13, 2025. https://www.reuters.com/business/retail-consumer/sonos-ceo-patrick-spence-steps-down-after-app-update-debacle-2025-01-13/.

Rogers, Everett M. *Diffusion of Innovations*. 5th edition. New York: Free Press, 2003.

Sanchez, Carlos. "Progressive Delivery in Kubernetes: Blue-Green and Canary Deployments." CloudBees, January 29, 2019. https://www.cloudbees.com/blog/progres-sive-delivery-kubernetes-blue-green-and-canary-deployments.

Sanders, Laura. "Slime Mold Grows Network Just Like Tokyo Rail System." WIRED, January 22, 2010. https://www.wired.com/2010/01/slime-mold-grows-network-just-like-tokyo-rail-system/.

Spool, Jared M. "The Quiet Death of the Major Re-Launch." UX Articles by Center Centre, March 11, 2016. https://articles.centercentre.com/death_of_relaunch/.

Targett, Edward. "Warren Buffett's GEICO Repatriates Work From the Cloud." The Stack, December 13, 2024. https://www.thestack.technology/warren-buffetts-ge-ico-repatriates-work-from-the-cloud-continues-ambitious-infrastructure-over-haul/.

Toffler, Alvin. *Future Shock*. New York: Random House, 1970.

"Total Number of Websites - Internet Live Stats." Accessed March 17, 2025. https://www.internetlivestats.com/total-number-of-websites/.

Wang, Sarah, Martin Casado, Peter Levine, and Sonal Chokshi. "The Cost of Cloud, a Trillion Dollar Paradox." Andreessen Horowitz, May 9, 2024. https://a16z.com/the-cost-of-cloud-a-trillion-dollar-paradox/.

"Well-Architected Framework: Design Principles." AWS. Accessed March 14, 2025. https://docs.aws.amazon.com/wellarchitected/latest/framework/cost-dp.html.

NOTES

Introduction

1. Dr. Cat Hicks, personal communication with the authors, May 2025.
2. Thomas Dohmke, personal communication with the authors, June 2025.

Chapter 1

1. Toffler, *Future Shock*, 10.
2. Rogers, *Diffusion of Innovations*.
3. Moore, *Crossing the Chasm*.
4. Sanchez, "Progressive Delivery in Kubernetes."
5. Pink, *Drive*.
6. Mills and Maslach, "Why We're Burned Out."
7. Spool, "The Quiet Death of the Major Re-Launch."

Chapter 2

1. Moore, "Cramming More Components."
2. Beck et al., "Manifesto for Agile Software Development."
3. Humble and Farley, *Continuous Delivery*.
4. "Blue-Green Deployment," GitLab.
5. "Design Principles," AWS.
6. Reuters, "Sonos CEO Patrick Spence Steps Down."
7. "What Is FinOps?," FinOps Foundation.
8. "What Is FinOps?," FinOps Foundation.
9. Wang et al., "The Cost of Cloud."
10. Targett, "Warren Buffett's GEICO Repatriates Work."

Chapter 3

1. Bruno Kurtic and Christian Beedgen, Zoom interview with James Governor, February 2025.

Chapter 4

1. Liker, *The Toyota Way*.
2. Humble and Farley, *Continuous Delivery*.
3. Knight Capital Americas LLC, "Order Instituting Administrative And Cease-And-Desist Proceedings."
4. *The Lego Movie*, directed by Lord and Miller.
5. Bazen, "Cell Phone Statistics 2025."
6. Atlassian, "State of the Developer Report."
7. Maslach and Jackson, "The Measurement of Experienced Burnout."
8. DORA, "Accelerate: State of DevOps 2018."
9. Marquet, *Turn the Ship Around!*
10. IT Revolution, "Leadership Development and Balancing Creativity."
11. Department of the Navy, "The Commanding Officer."
12. Edmondson, *The Fearless Organization*.
13. Hicks, "Psychological Affordances."
14. DORA, "Accelerate: State of DevOps 2018."

Chapter 5

1. All quotes from the GitHub Case study by Sam Lambert are from an interview recorded over Zoom between Sam Lambert and James Governor in December 2024.
2. Chacon, "GitHub Flow."

Chapter 6

1. Majors, "So You Want to Build an Observability Tool."
2. Puppet Labs, IT Revolution Press, and ThoughtWorks, "2014 State of DevOps Report."
3. Lovelace, *Ada, the Enchantress of Numbers*.

Chapter 7

1. All quotes in this case study are taken directly from an in-person interview between Brian Scott and Adam Zimman in August 2024.

Chapter 8

1. Sanders, "Slime Mold Grows Network."
2. Evans, "What Happens When You Press a Key."

3. McLeod, "Harry Harlow Monkey Experiments."

Chapter 9

1. All quotes in this case study are from a recorded interview between James Governor, Deepak Singh, and Clare Ligouri that was recorded in September 2024.

Chapter 10

1. IT Revolution, "Change in a Successful Organization."
2. DORA, "Accelerate: State of DevOps 2024."
3. "Gartner Hype Cycle Research Methodology," Gartner.
4. Henshall, "When Might AI Outsmart Us?"

Chapter 11

1. Kuang, "Disney's $1 Billion Bet on a Magical Wristband."
2. Cox, "Disney Global SRE – Creating Digital Magic," 2022.
3. C. "How Disney Uses Digital Twins to Maintain Its Most Innovative Rides."
4. Cox, "Disney Global SRE – Creating Digital Magic," 2023.
5. Cox, "Disney Global SRE – Creating Digital Magic," 2023.
6. Cox, "Disney Global SRE – Creating Digital Magic," 2022.
7. Cox, "Disney Global SRE – Creating Digital Magic," 2022.
8. Cox, "Disney Global SRE – Creating Digital Magic," 2023.

Chapter 12

1. Lufkin, "The Curious Origins of Online Shopping."
2. "Total Number of Websites," Internet Live Stats.
3. "Nike (NKE) - Market Capitalization."
4. All quotes from Ron Forrester are from an interview with the authors conducted via video call, April 7, 2023.
5. All quotes from Sam Gordon are from an interview with the authors conducted via video call, April 7, 2023.
6. "NikeID: Polishing the Shoe Buying Experience."
7. Toffler, *Future Shock*, 2.
8. Megginson, "Lessons from Europe for American Business," 4.

ACKNOWLEDGMENTS

James Governor

Thanks to Istio, for inspiring me to see new development patterns that led me to create a new industry term.

Thanks to Sam Guckenheimer, who helped kick all this off with a throw-away comment about how Microsoft tests stuff.

Thanks to Stefan Prodan, who built Flagger, the first tool designed for Progressive Delivery.

Thanks to Alexis Richardson—my bestie. Always thoughtful about GitOps, Progressive Delivery, and observability.

Thanks to the team at RedMonk who have helped make the time and space for me to work on this—with special thanks to Rachel Stephens for her close reading of the text and unflagging support.

Thanks to Adam, Kim, and Heidi, my coauthors, who made the book happen. Amazing people—all smarts, kindness, and tolerance. The kind of people I would always want to hang out with.

Thanks to Natalie, who puts up with me. And the kids—they're pretty awesome.

Thanks to IT Revolution—we always had you in mind as the publishers, so it's awesome to have a book go out with you. Anna and Leah—take a bow.

Thanks to all the folks who have contributed to the ideas in the book, who agreed that Progressive Delivery made sense, who are building products to support it, who talked about it in keynotes and webinars, and who invited me to talk to their customers about it.

Thanks to folks like Charity Majors, Dave Carow, and Carlos Sanchez, who, quite simply, get it.

Kim Harrison

Thank you, Jorge, for taking care of me. You always made sure I took breaks, ate food, got outside, and remembered to have fun. Your excitement and support throughout this project made all the difference.

Thank you, friends and family, for letting me talk endlessly about this project. You all feigned interest, even if I went deep on some of the driest parts of the story. I can't tell you how much I appreciate you cheering me on and being so excited for this.

Thank you, fellow authors; it's been an absolute pleasure working on this project with you. Our weekly sessions have been one of my favorite parts of the week.

Thank you to our editors. You took our story and made it bigger and stronger. You were so patient and gracious with us throughout the process.

Thank you, peer reviewers. You made time to read through this material and give us honest, heartfelt feedback. Your insights helped us strengthen the story, and it wouldn't be the same without you.

Heidi Waterhouse

A deep and heartfelt thank you to my wife, Megan, for being the kind of helpmate who makes creative work possible.

Thank you to my kids, Sebastian and Carolyn, for talking about both "your book" and "your next book."

To my family of origin, especially my parents, who have cheerfully encouraged all their offspring to be as insatiably curious as the elephant's child, and who were the source of many of the history bits in this book, at least indirectly.

Thank you to my weird systers of all genders who live in my pocket and help me hammer out thorny problems, especially Lilly and Rose and Rachel and Cat and Gus and Sumana.

Thank you to my favorite grumpy sysadmin, Laura, for reminding me all the time about technical work in a world without silly valley money.

The teachers were right when they told us that the working world is full of group projects. I am so happy I finally get to pick my own groups. Thank you to my coauthors, who have made the dream of teamwork real.

There are dozens of people who made this book better by talking through ideas with me or by reviewing posts and drafts. I am indebted to them.

Finally, thank you to the women who walked before me, like Ruth Cowan, Kathy Sierra, Donella Meadows, Marianne Bellotti, Nicole Forsgren, Dominica DeGrandis, and Lillian Gilbreth. I am because you are.

Adam Zimman

To my wife, Kate, thank you for your never-ending support, encouragement, and partnership in all the things.

To Ez, for being the source of my initial inspiration for Progressive Delivery and a constant reminder that change is easier when you have a mentor. And your playlists...endless musical motivation.

To Milo, for teaching me all about iterative building and collaboration through thousands of LEGO® builds and our ten-year-old Minecraft world.

To Marilyn, Bob, Judy, and Leo, for reminding me that getting old is hard and adapting to change is a logarithmic challenge.

To Carolyn and Ari, the teachers who empowered me to have the confidence to write a book even with dyslexia and dysgraphia.

To my coauthors, thank you for the weekly therapy working sessions, partnership, and incredible friendship. I'm a better writer and a better human because of my time with you all.

And Inigo, for the snuggles.

All of Us

We couldn't have done this without the spectacular team at IT Revolution who took an idea we'd been working on and helped us make it actionable and usable. Thank you to our reviewers, including Cat Hicks, Rachel Stephens, Nathen Harvey, Hazel Weakly, Rachel Chalmers, Aneel Lakhani, Paul

Hammond, Jessica Kerr, Katie McLaughlin, Betty Junod, Pat Lee, Susan Gudenkauf, Matt Ring, Jason Cox, Brian Scott, Kent Beck, Ron Forrester, Sam Gordon, Sam Lambert, Deepak Singh, Claire Liguori, and Christian Beedgen.

ABOUT THE AUTHORS

James Governor is the cofounder of RedMonk, the only developer-focused industry analyst firm. He advises clients on practitioner-led technology adoption and engineering, project management, open source, and community and technology strategy. Governor is credited as having coined the term "Progressive Delivery." Vermouth advocate. He lives in London.

Kimberly Harrison is a sociologist focused on the development and adoption of new technology within the software industry. She enjoys working with early-stage startups that are developing new tools and methodologies for modern development teams. She specializes in strategic communications and community building. She lives in the San Francisco Bay area.

Heidi Waterhouse spent a couple of decades as a technical writer at Microsoft, Dell Software, LaunchDarkly, and many, many startups, learning to communicate with and for developers. She coauthored *Docs for Developers: An Engineer's Field Guide to Technical Writing*. She is passionate about storytelling, finding business value, and the ROI of laptop stickers. When she's not helping craft startup messaging, you can find her in her sewing room listening to a book. She lives in Minneapolis, Minnesota.

Adam Zimman is a startup and venture capital adviser providing guidance on leadership, platform architecture, product marketing, and GTM strategy. He has over twenty years of experience working in a variety of roles from software engineering to technical sales. He has worked in both enterprise and consumer companies such as VMware, EMC, GitHub, and LaunchDarkly. Adam is driven by a passion for inclusive leadership and solving problems with technology. As an adviser, he works with a number of startups and nonprofits. His perspective on life has been shaped by a background in physics and visual art, an ongoing adventure as a husband and father, and a childhood career as a fire juggler. He lives with his family in the San Francisco Bay area.